CU00937780

This book is for you if...

- you have lost a loved one unexpectedly, and you want to know how to overcome the unbearable pain

- you have experienced other traumatic losses in your life

- you would like to learn more about the life lessons, processes and strategies to help you through difficult periods in your life

- you love real-life stories and memoirs

- you are searching for inspiration and motivation

- you are considering a journey of healing to help yourself and others

- you need to release yourself from feelings of self-doubt that hold you back

- you want to immerse yourself in a journey of self-discovery, growth and acceptance

- you want to learn how to move forward with your life

- you are hoping for a thought-provoking read

"Written from the heart! Hooked from the beginning, I went from pining for days gone by, to empathy and tears, and finally joy for my friend ('The Cas Lass gone good') who didn't just survive trauma, but found her way to happiness and fulfilment.

Yvonne shares a tumultuous personal journey in a compelling, relatable, authentic way. A rare, humorous and inspirational page turner. Yvonne skilfully shares her own life lessons ('Yvonne's Top Tips') and uses a wonderful vocabulary to evoke detailed imagery and engaging stories."

Kate Osborne
Mindfulness Trainer and Results Trained Coach

◊◊◊◊◊

"They say that what doesn't kill you makes you stronger, and Yvonne epitomises that phrase over and over again. Trauma, loss, divorce, health issues, dealing with deprivation and more, this lady has been there and got the T-shirt!

I've known Yvonne for many years and didn't know half of what she has written in her book. I'd sum it up by saying it is a handbook for life, and I love the snippets of wisdom at the end of each chapter.

Having authored myself, this doubtless has been a cathartic and healing process for Yvonne, and I know it will help so many people. Well done!"

Colin Tansley
Author of *Mastering the Wolf* and
The Little Book of Wolfie Wisdom

"A searingly honest account of an ordinary woman's life, who through sheer hard work and determination has turned her life around and become a successful businesswoman following a devastating forced adoption at just 15 years old.

The basic principle of learning how to love and value yourself before others is a life lesson; hard to learn but, once grasped, proves vital.

A thought-provoking story if you are willing to be honest with yourself; you may well find answers to questions you didn't realise you were looking for.

Good luck with the book, Vonnie!"

Tracey
Retired Police Officer

◊◊◊◊◊

"Are you one of them? There are so many people that would benefit from reading this book. Would you like to feel happier, have more confidence, and learn to like and understand yourself?

The author has laid her soul bare, giving total transparency of her life. It is a journey from a happy childhood to traumatic teenage years through to the responsibilities of adult and parenthood. Despite many struggles and setbacks, she has risen to the top of her profession and found happiness in all aspects of her life. A truly inspirational read."

Christine Ivel
An avid reader who is very proud of
her friend The Cas Lass

"I have so much admiration for Yvonne writing this book as she has been open and honest, telling what is an extremely moving account of her life and family.

Yvonne has not been afraid to tackle subjects that are uncomfortable to deal with, and she does not shy away from the after-effects of what she had to deal with.

Having worked with Yvonne, she has used all of her experience to build a successful career and family life that she should be extremely proud of, and I am privileged to know her."

Janet Shreeve
Mother, Grandmother, Business Owner and Director

◊◊◊◊◊

"*Memory Boxes* is a thought-provoking book, rooted in truth and family. It demonstrates Yvonne's bravery, passion, vulnerability, pain, and resilience. She is not afraid to admit to missteps and misjudgement, which makes it an absorbing, refreshing memoir.

Memory Boxes is utterly heartbreaking yet uplifting, and will linger in your mind long after you have read it."

Olivia Eisinger
Freelance Editor and Proofreader

One Woman's Story of
Forced Adoption, Loss and Self-Loathing

Memory Boxes

Illuminating a Path to Happiness

Yvonne Tomlinson

First published in Great Britain in 2024
by Book Brilliance Publishing
265A Fir Tree Road, Epsom, Surrey, KT17 3LF
United Kingdom
+44 (0)20 8641 5090
www.bookbrilliancepublishing.com
admin@bookbrilliancepublishing.com

© Copyright Yvonne Tomlinson 2024

The moral right of Yvonne Tomlinson to be identified as
the author of this work has been asserted in accordance
with the Copyright, Designs and Patents Acts 1988.

All rights reserved. No part of this publication may be
reproduced, stored in a retrieval system, or transmitted,
in any form or by any means without the prior written
permission of the publisher, nor be otherwise circulated
in any form of binding or cover than that in which it is
published and without similar condition being imposed
on the subsequent purchaser.

A CIP catalogue record for this book is available
at the British Library.

ISBN 978-1-913770-86-0

This book is memoir.
It reflects the author's present recollections of experiences
over time. Some names and characteristics have been
changed, some events have been compressed, and some
dialogue has been recreated.

This book is dedicated to my Grandad Fred,
a hard working miner whose unconditional love
never wavered.

Contents

Foreword

Memory Boxes is a book by a true Yorkshire woman and will be enjoyed by all Yorkshire and Northern women in particular. Yvonne Tomlinson's description of her family, her community, her experience of school life, marriage, divorce, love and loss, told in the words and cadence of a Northern woman, will resonate with many Northerners, especially with working class backgrounds. Her descriptions of personal and family tragedy, and coming to terms with them, will also resonate – but most especially with those who share her culture and heritage.

The theme that runs throughout the book, etched into the narrative as it is etched into her life, is the removal of her son at birth, and the silence that then surrounded this heart-wrenching experience. This is the tragedy that defines Memory Boxes and around which all the other themes coalesce. It even defines the structure of the book, as she metaphorically boxes up this memory as a teenager and puts it away, and continues to box up her other memories. It is on writing the book that she finally opens the boxes and reflects on her memories.

Nevertheless, it is clear that although this terrible event has left an indelible mark on her life, she is not defined by it; she comes from a close knit family, full of love and joy. She has experienced deeply fulfilling life partnerships, has excelled in her work, enjoys golf and friendships, and dotes on her children and grandchildren. This is a life well-lived in and amongst the tragedies that come to us all. In this way, the story is both her story and everyone's story – and this is its deep attraction.

Reading *Memory Boxes* is like sitting down with your girlfriends one long sunny afternoon with a bottle of Prosecco (or two!) and sharing stories about each others' lives. The book has a warm, homely feel about ordinary people's lives and the wisdom of living, loving and learning. The extraordinary in the ordinary, the joys and sorrows of living, the determination and the love to find your path from the dark places, to come to terms with your greatest tragedies and, like the air, rise.

The word that comes to mind is cherish – a woman and a book to cherish. Thank you for sharing your story, Yvonne; I raise my glass to you, and wish you and your family well.

Ruth Weston
Social Entrepreneur, Birth & Maternity Services Activist and Campaigner

Why?

Dear Reader:

For years I had unanswered questions that nobody could help me with. Locking memories away in the box within my brain was easy, but it wasn't the answer – I didn't know that at the time.

For those of you who are going through difficult times, I don't have all the answers; I don't even have all my own answers but I do, however, have my own personal learning. We go through many things in life that change the direction of our path. My direction was changed at the age of 15, with innocence gone and a change that had a long-lasting effect on my life.

Those around me were unaware. Masterful at wearing a mask, I hid my emotions, the smile on my face covering many a true feeling.

I tried on many occasions to move on and to forget. However, one day, out of the blue, a television programme triggered a memory that made the mask slip – tears flowed and my mood altered. This was alien to me.

Opening up to someone is a starting point, but I couldn't open up to those closest to me. Fortunately, friends persuaded me and pointed me in the right direction. Asking for help is hard, but once you have done so, it gets easier; you learn to cope, to understand, and to make choices.

My choice was to let my past eat away at me and take me down a long and dark tunnel. Luckily, I discovered a hidden strength, deep within the recesses of my mind and soul, that was supported by my ex-husband, current partner, friends and children. They were and are my sense of reality which I will always remember. They didn't judge me, but gave me strength.

Why Am I Writing This Book?

I want to help others to understand that we are all individuals; our life experiences make us the person we are. Acknowledgement doesn't happen overnight. To get to where you want to be takes time, honesty and transparency.

Contraversally, forgiveness is not always required; you don't always need to forgive others and you don't need to forgive yourself.

I am truly happy with my life. It has been a journey, no, rephrase that – it IS a journey, a journey of learning, emotions, understanding, acknowledgement of the happy times, the sad times, and the everyday lifetimes.

Yvonne

Memory Box 1: Childhood

Nostalgic Echoes of Innocence

Play

In the golden haze of memory, I revisit those long, sun-drenched summer days of childhood. The 1960s was a time when the neighbourhood street transformed into a playground, and the only rule was to play until the sun dipped below the horizon. It was an era where the dirt on your skin was a badge of resilience, a shield against the invisible foes that hovered in the background. Climbing trees, crafting toys from anything we could lay our hands on, indulging in games of hide and seek, and kicking a ball in the middle of the street were rites of passage, unencumbered by thoughts of risk.

In those days, my mother's hair blazed like a flame, and she exuded youth and vitality. Frolicking under the evening sun, I often found myself curious about the conversations shared by the mothers while we kids revelled in the freedom of the outdoors. Our street saw only sporadic traffic and was a safe haven.

I recall the art of skipping, a skill my mother taught me, turning a simple washing line into a makeshift skipping rope. The rhythmic twining of the rope by the mothers at either end created a makeshift arena for our exuberant jumps. Bumps and grazes were the currency of our play, earned as our feet tangled with the skipping rope, sending us tumbling to the ground. And as the evening drew to a close, fatigue battled with our reluctance to surrender to bedtime.

The 1970s bestowed upon us endless summer days, a time when the outdoors trumped the allure of the television screen. Computers and electronic games were not for the likes of us; our entertainment was forged in the practicality and ingenuity of building go-karts with scavenged pram wheels and discarded wood. Johnny and Shawn, the local go-kart virtuosos, transformed our mundane afternoons into thrilling races along the pavement, with no hint of the backaches that plague modern sedentary pursuits.

Kites soared in the azure sky, fashioned from plastic bags, string and canes, masterfully crafted by my dad. Our kites became loyal companions, accompanying us wherever we roamed. Life was simple, and happiness was measured by the love shared among us.

My younger brother, Martin, affectionately nicknamed Ginger Babby by our parents, mirrored my every step. The self-appointed strong and bossy big sister, I inadvertently led him down the paths of scraped knees and teary escapades. Yet, our bond was unbreakable, a testament to the shared adventures and occasional mishaps.

Amid this innocence, a daredevil spirit beckoned. I became the 'tomboy,' thirsty for excitement. That's what we called girls before the millennium who played with boys, and preferred the rough and tumble of boys' games rather than dolls. Martin, my faithful companion, followed in my footsteps, both figuratively and literally. His admiration was evident as he attempted to climb a tree after witnessing my fearless ascent. Predictably, he would tumble, tears and scraped knees the price of his daring imitation. Guilt cloaked me briefly; after all, as the elder sister, I should have known better. Yet, our childhood mischief carried on, oblivious to the consequences that loomed in the shadows.

One particular year stands out vividly, a time when we resided in the suburb of Airedale, in Yorkshire. Our three-bedroomed council house witnessed the whims of innocence. The streets echoed with children's laughter, untethered by the constraints of traffic, watched over only by nosy neighbours. A kite-flying escapade took an unexpected turn when Martin lost control, and our prized possession hitched a ride on a passing double-decker bus! Laughter turned to dismay as the bus carried our kite away, and we chased it down the road in futile pursuit. The consequences of our escapade were inconsequential then; we were free spirits, undeterred by the unforeseen risks of our adventures.

In those bygone days, our journeys were guided not by GPS but by familiar landmarks. The garage, with its adjacent sweet shop, served as our North Star. Crossing main roads at a tender age, I felt the rush of independence. The sweet shop, a treasure trove of delights, beckoned with its jars filled with sugary wonders. Watching the sweets tip onto the scales, the sound of their measured weight in ounces, held a certain magic. A sixpence could buy me black chews and monkey nuts, timeless treats that still evoke the flavours of my youth. The memory of blackened teeth and sticky smiles remains, a testament to a time when innocence was savoured and pleasures were simple.

In the symphony of recollections, these fragments of childhood innocence composed the overture to a life marked by simplicity, camaraderie, and the boundless joy of unfettered play.

The Forgotten Stroll
In the Shadows of Innocence

Let's journey back further into the recesses of my childhood, a time when my brother was confined to the safety of his pram, cocooned in the embrace of our seemingly idyllic neighbourhood. It was an era when Mum felt an unwavering sense of security as she manoeuvred the world with a pram, a symbol of maternal devotion.

On a routine day, we embarked on a pilgrimage to the local Co-op, a mere 15-minute walk from our house. I clung to the pram's handle, its robust wheels propelling us forward, while Martin, still in his infancy, nestled within its protective confines. The Co-op, a realm of necessity, awaited us. However, the pram's width denied us entry into the shop, prompting Mum to engage the brake and assign me the role of guardian.

With steadfast determination, Mum delved into the aisles, acquiring the essentials for our modest household. Oblivious to the passage of time, she returned home, only to be greeted by a nagging voice in her head – a maternal sixth sense alerting her to a crucial oversight. A realisation struck: she had left us at the Co-op, frozen in place, tethered to the pram like forgotten sentinels! The anecdote flickers in my memory, a tale recounted through the years by Mum, a testament to her knack for transforming a mishap into a cherished family narrative.

The move to a new home from the council house in Airedale to a newly-built housing estate just on the outskirts of Castleford town centre at the tender age of seven marked the end of an era. Childhood innocence slipped away, and the familiar rhythms of play transformed. Mum, once a participant in our outdoor escapades, withdrew from the merriment. New friendships blossomed, and with an unabated spirit, I embraced the label of a tomboy. In an era devoid of today's gender norms, we engaged in clandestine adventures – leaping off stacks of bricks, constructing secret forts in the woods, and vanishing for hours with a simple jam sandwich as our sustenance.

Amid the transition, a lasting gift from Dad emerged – an intricately crafted remote-controlled balsa wood boat, a testament to parental love and attention. Rediscovering the boat in the recesses of Mum and Dad's loft years later, with my childhood nickname Vonnie delicately painted on its side, evoked a surge of sentimentality.

Memories resurfaced of Pontefract Park's boating lake, where Dad, with masterful control, set the boat adrift, eliciting awe from my young eyes. However, fate intervened as the boat found itself marooned on the lake's central island. Undeterred, Dad commandeered a paddle boat, navigating the waters to rescue the stranded vessel. However, his bold rescue incurred the park keeper's wrath, a lesson in questionable ethics for us children. Nevertheless, the boat, cradled in Dad's arms, returned to me – a symbol of love, adventure, and a father's willingness to bend the rules for his daughter's happiness.

Today, as I gaze upon the boat in my bedroom, its presence radiates warmth and elicits tears – tears for a bygone childhood and the enduring warmth of a father's love etched in every detail.

In the mosaic of memories, the most precious fragments are those crafted with thought and love, far greater than the allure of expensive trinkets or digital diversions. They are the treasures of a cherished past, where innocence thrived, and the heart found solace in the simplest gestures of affection.

Treasured Moments with Grandparents
Roots and Reverie

In the 1960s, Martin and I were the sole grandchildren – a notion that unfurls a tapestry woven with warmth, love, and the humble origins of our family legacy. As the years unfolded, a tale emerged, a tale whispered in the winds of time about the morning of my birth – a morning that saw Grandad Fred, with unbridled joy, venturing into the streets to collect horse manure from a passing steed, an earthy tribute to becoming a grandfather.

My heart beats with great fondness of recollections of Grandad Fred's garden, a sprawling canvas of beauty that he nurtured with a miner's hands and a grandfather's love. Amidst the green expanse, there lay a mosaic – a fruit and vegetable plot, a fragrant flower bed, a verdant grassy haven, an area for animals, and, at its heart, a clay bed where childhood dreams took root. When not engulfed in the depths of the coal mine, Grandad, a stoic figure, found solace in his rocking chair, pipe in hand, crafting whimsical pipe cleaner figures for the children.

Hours unfolded in the garden, Grandad patiently guiding me through the nuances of cultivation, from seed to table. The bounty of his labour, vibrant green beans and earthy beetroots, found their way to our family dinners, thanks to his devoted care. In the greenhouse, tomatoes thrived, and a shed, a realm of mystery, stood as a silent witness to his tireless efforts.

Much like my parents, Nanna and Grandad navigated life with modest means, their wealth measured not in coins but in a hothouse fuelled by abundant coal. Chocolate, a sweet indulgence, lay hidden beneath the stairs, a reminder of Nanna's part-time tenure at the chocolate factory. Despite the financial constraints, their home exuded an abundance of love.

Later revelations unfolded the depth of their love, etched in the fabric of daily life in Castleford, where they spent every moment together. Grandad would converse with pals outside the shops, while Nanna embarked on the weekly quest for groceries. Their bond remained unbroken until Nanna's passing, a revelation that underscored the sacrifices made in the name of love.

Sundays ushered in cherished rituals – a family drive, a visit to Nanna and Grandad's, and the pungent aroma of cigarettes in the car. Fairburn Ings became a haven for our Sunday escapades, where ducks, geese and swans awaited our arrival with theatrical displays of excitement. Memories crystallised of walks in the woods near Selby, where autumn leaves crunched beneath our feet and conkers found refuge in eager pockets.

In this swirl of adventures, a daring note emerged – the thrill of sitting on my dad's motorbike as a young girl, a forbidden joy in today's safety-conscious era. Dad, a dual wielder of motorbike and car, navigated the roads while Mum, the navigator sans GPS, occasionally sparked arguments over directional prowess...

Post-adventures, Dad's mysterious 'church' visits to drink 'holy water' at the pub paved the way for Sunday afternoons steeped in 1960's melodies, with Mum's voice harmonising to the tunes of Elvis Presley.

Sunday lunches unfolded as a hearty tradition – soggy vegetables, slow-cooked joints, and tantalising aromas wafting through the house. The bone-in meat became a coveted prize, sparking playful arguments between Martin and me. Yorkshire puddings and gravy graced the table, a testament to this Yorkshire girl's unwavering love for the savoury elixir.

Family time gelled around the Sunday lunch table, a tradition untouched by time. Post-feast, Mum and Dad succumbed to the afternoon siesta, while Martin and I revelled in play. An uncomplicated tea of sandwiches and tinned mixed fruit with Carnation cream capped off the day – a simple symphony of familial love and enduring traditions.

The Tapestry of Grandparental Love
Cherished Moments and Nurturing Arms

Growing up in the embrace of my grandparents was a privilege, a treasure woven into the fabric of my existence that continues to shimmer to this day, with the glow of nostalgia. Whenever thoughts of my grandparents envelop me, a warmth unfurls within, especially when I delve into the reservoir of memories from the holidays we spent together.

In the mosaic of our two families – Nanna, Grandad, my aunty and uncles – we embarked on camping escapades that unfurled across the countryside. The journey to our holiday haven, often stretching for hours, wasn't my favourite, but was sweetened by rounds of I spy and

Dad's singing. He was a talented singer and musician who made sure music accompanied us wherever we ventured.

My fondest recollections are around the camping grounds perched on Whitby's clifftops along the North Yorkshire coast or the sun-soaked beaches of Tenby in South Wales. Reflecting on those times, I marvel at the magical feat of fitting everything – canvas tents, heavy poles, duvet-sized sleeping bags, camping stoves, pots, pans, and more – into a seemingly compact Hillman Imp, a mini and two small trailers. It was, without a doubt, a camping Tardis, considering the bulky and cumbersome nature of camping gear in the 1960s and 1970s.

Days unfolded in simple joy, playing on the beach and braving the cold embrace of the North Sea. Nights brought the delight of pop and crisps, while Dad and Grandad ventured off to the pub. Card games, with a dash of well-executed cheating, added an extra layer of amusement to our carefree existence – a life underscored by simplicity, happiness and unbridled fun.

Tenby, with its incredible night-time thunderstorms, offered indelible memories. As hot days surrendered to the symphony of thunder, I'd watch fork lightning dance across the distant sea from the safety of our tents. Those summers, it seemed, were destined to last forever.

The sanctuary of familial love embraced me throughout my childhood. Dad's little girl, I perched on his knee, serenaded by a song that echoed my nickname, *My Bonnie Lies Over the Ocean*.[1] A sweet smile dances on my lips to this day whenever the melody graces my thoughts. With long blonde hair and blue eyes, the term 'big-boned' lingered, but in Dad's eyes, I was his cherished Bonnie.

Our family, though numerically four, felt much larger. Nanna and Grandad, residing not far away with an aunt and uncles of varying ages, blurred the lines between households. Early childhood unfolded in the shared embrace of Nanna and Mum, a harmonious partnership woven across different roofs, but under the same familial umbrella.

Our humble abode, a council house with its share of cold, mice and peculiar neighbours, held a warmth that transcended physical discomforts. Mum's ingenious warmth trick – wrapping the coal fire's back plate in a pillowcase before placing it in our beds – rendered bedtime a sanctuary of comfort amid the chill! Heavy layers of sheets and blankets cocooned us in layers of warmth.

Grandad Fred, a timeless presence, inhabits the depth of my memories. There he is in his rocking chair, the tendrils of pipe smoke wafting through the air. His pride and joy, the garden, stood testament to his unwavering dedication, each scar etched on his body narrating a tale of hard work and resilience. Perching on his knee, absorbing tales of cowboy and Indian battles and shark escapades, I was enveloped in the warmth of his pipe smoke – a scent that, to this day, lingers as a cherished memory. He was not just warm; he was love personified, understanding and endlessly proud.

As the eldest grandchild, I basked in the spoils of affection and adoration that he showered upon me, a legacy that continues to illuminate my heart.

Christmas Unveiled

For me, Christmas has always been an exquisite time woven with threads of magic – a childhood wonder that has seamlessly transcended into the realms of today. The expansive kinship that embraced grandparents, aunties and uncles made every Christmas a symphony of shared joy. In our house in the 1960s, where financial constraints were the norm, Christmas wasn't adorned with commercial excesses, but was simple and authentic. The days leading up to Christmas were filled with the excitement of crafting letters to Santa.

On Christmas Eve, our house bore no festive adornments; no tree graced the living room. It was a canvas awaiting the brushstrokes of enchantment. As we drifted into slumber, a sense of anticipation hung in the air. On Christmas morning, our eyes fluttered open to the sight of stockings at the foot of our beds – a treasure trove of fruit, nuts and coins – an unmistakable sign that the jolly man in the red suit had visited us!

Stepping into the living room was a journey into a surreal kingdom. Not content with just delivering gifts, Santa had transformed our space into a twinkling wonderland. Foiled trimmings cascaded across the room, converging in the centre. Glass baubles, tinsel and lights adorned a small artificial tree – a sparkling spectacle that fuelled our childhood delight. One particular Christmas, when I was about seven, my heart held a wish, an unmet desire that lingered even after the presents were unwrapped.

My mum, sensing my lingering disappointment, directed me to the pantry – an unsuspecting treasure trove. And there it was, my dream Christmas present, a Bontempi organ! The elation of that moment stayed with me, a cherished memory woven into the fabric of my childhood. From sitting on my dad's knee singing timeless tunes, to mastering melodies on the organ, it became a musical journey that transcended generations.

The rhythm of Christmas followed a traditional cadence. After unwrapping our gifts at home, we set forth to visit both sets of grandparents, the excitement of more gifts awaiting us there. Returning home for lunch, the kitchen was Mum's domain, while Dad embarked on his ritual pub visit – the 'Church' as he fondly called it! The table was graced with the quintessential festive feast – turkey, stuffing, roast potatoes and a symphony of vegetables. My favourite, a rich fruit Christmas pudding, followed, though Mum insisted on modest portion sizes.

Post-feast, we huddled around the television, the Queen's speech heralding a moment of national unity. A film, etched in memory, often *The Wizard of Oz*[2], filled our Christmas afternoons. While Mum and Dad dozed off, we engaged in the magic of our new toys.

Yet, as much as Christmas Day held its enchantment, the real spectacle unfolded on Boxing Day – a household teeming with life. Nanna and Grandad's home became the epicentre, a gathering of family, aunts, uncles and an ever-growing family of cousins, for the remnants of Christmas feasts, a delightful assortment of leftover meats, pork pies, pickles, sandwiches and homemade trifles. The front room, a battleground for the younger generation, witnessed wrestling matches, laughter and the camaraderie that bound me with my younger uncles and aunt. As we matured, Monopoly around a large table replaced the wrestling bouts, endured through heated bickering and laughter.

For a child, Christmas is a time filled with magic – the belief in Santa's nocturnal journey with his reindeer and a sleigh laden with gifts. The yuletide spirit emanated from the Christmas nativity, the carol concert, and the classroom adorned in festive colours. Yet, as the enchantment of Santa waned with age, Christmas transformed, shifting its focus from the anticipation of gifts to the joy of giving – a metamorphosis that echoed the evolution of the seasons and the passage of time.

Building Love Amidst Renovations
Home-Building Adventures

As the years unfolded, I found myself transitioning into young womanhood, navigating the intricate dance of life's milestones. At the heart of this Memory Box lies a story of commitment, a house full of dreams and the unexpected turns that shaped the foundation of our shared journey.

I recall the moment when my then-boyfriend Rob and I made a pact to stand side by side, not just in love but in bricks and mortar. The decision to invest in our first home was a testament to our dedication. An intriguing twist presented itself when he was offered an opportunity to go to Australia for a rugby extravaganza; this was tempting, dangling just within his reach. However, in a surprising turn of events, he chose a different path – he chose to invest that substantial sum in a home with me.

Our new-found dwelling, like many of its time, begged for a facelift. Uninhabitable in its current state, it cried out for a complete overhaul – new wiring, plumbing, plastering, and the seemingly essential transformation of an outdoor toilet into a domestic haven. The to-do list was exhaustive, and our days after work, weekends and holidays became a symphony of renovation. Every nook and cranny held the echoes of our determination and love.

However, I wasn't always the most adept assistant. On a particular day, tasked with loading scaffolding with bricks, I inadvertently turned the set-up into a precarious see-saw, a potential disaster in the making, averted only by Rob's timely intervention. In an attempt to redeem myself, I was reassigned to the 'safer' task of staining the skirting boards. The walls, freshly painted in Magnolia – bought in bulk to save costs – beckoned for their finishing touch. Alas, fate had different plans. A clumsy misstep and the expensive wood stain found a new home across those pristine walls... Rob's frustration was palpable, and my day took a downturn.

Frustrations escalated, reaching boiling point. In a fit of exasperation, he 'suggested' I retreat to the familiar haven of my parents' home. A journey home intertwined with yet another misstep – this time, a toppled wood pallet that found its mark on my beloved Ford Fiesta. A cascade of unfortunate events, marking a day etched in the annals of a Memory Box.

Amidst the challenges of renovation woes, Christmas dawned, accompanied by an unexpected and far-from-thrilling gift – a vacuum cleaner! Well, yippee! I wore my discontent like a heavy cloak, airing my grievances about the apparent injustice of 'house presents.' Sulking through the morning, I regaled my parents with tales of the ill-fated gift. Little did I know that the universe had a surprise in store.

Later that morning, as we exchanged gifts at Rob's parents' home, a moment unfolded that would redefine our journey. By the warmth of the fire, Rob, in a surprising twist, asked for my hand in marriage. A solitaire diamond ring, a perfect fit, suddenly appeared! He had taken one of the rings I rarely wore so wouldn't notice it was gone, and had used the sizing system at the jewellers – a proposal shrouded in secrecy, planned with precision, and a question poised in the midst of holiday cheer. The vacuum cleaner became an afterthought, and I found myself saying yes to a future built not only on renovations, but on the enduring promise of love.

The Evolution of Christmas Joy

When my children were born, there was a significant shift from the nostalgia of my childhood festivities. The joy of gifting and enchanting my daughters brought a fresh, vibrant energy to the season, adding to our family home of love and merriment.

The countdown to Christmas wasn't confined to the Eve, but unfurled on the first of December with the unveiling of the advent calendar. Each day's door revealed a morsel of chocolate, a precursor to the grand spectacle awaiting us. Our home adorned itself with festive cheer approximately two weeks before Christmas, a meticulous process that involved planning presents months in advance. We often found ourselves with an excess of gifts, making the art of concealment, wrapping and assembling toys a logistical challenge.

Christmas Eve became a magical prelude, with our girls donning new Christmas pyjamas, leaving out carrots and milk for Santa and his reindeer. Coaxing them into sleep was an art as their excitement bubbled over. One memorable Christmas involved a clever ruse with our eldest, Emma. She had inadvertently missed a day on her advent calendar, unknowingly prolonging the anticipation. The unintended consequence was a Christmas morning that failed to unfold with the expected enthusiasm. Lesson learned, and in the subsequent years, we diligently opened the advent calendar each day, preserving the excitement that was uniquely Christmas Eve.

As our girls matured, the desire to relish their presents led us to establish a new tradition – Christmas dinner at home. Breakfast at my parents', a festive feast at our place, and a late afternoon visit to my in-laws became the cherished itinerary. Evenings saw the adults gathered around a table laden with homemade buffets, a post-feast bonanza with tempting offerings. The children and their cousins indulged in play, and the night would eventually culminate in shared laughter and repose.

Boxing Day, once a reflection of my childhood, transformed into a day of domestic cocooning. The children revelled in their new toys, and we attempted to conquer the remnants of an overstuffed refrigerator. My penchant for excess, a vestige of scarcity from childhood, manifested into an abundance of festive provisions. The landscape had changed from the days of closed shops and scarcity; now, convenience stores beckoned for any forgotten items.

Battery-operated toys, some noisier than one could fathom, made their presence known. A quiet night was often achieved by surreptitiously removing the batteries, citing a mundane 'technical glitch' to justify the sudden silence…

The magic of Christmas with my children held a profound charm, fuelled by the cultivation of belief in Father Christmas. Witnessing the sparkle in their eyes and the contagious excitement as they unwrapped presents encapsulated the essence of the season. However, once my children inevitably outgrew the enchantment, later a new chapter unfolded – the joy of witnessing the same wonder in my grandchildren.

Christmas has always been about family unity for me. Understanding the delicate balance of familial ties on Christmas Day, nowadays we gather before the festivities, granting our children the freedom to choose their own Christmas path. Christmas morning emerges as a harmonious convergence at my mum's, where four generations share the magic before embarking on individual journeys.

Yet, amidst the festive joy, I confronted my most challenging Christmas, finding myself alone for the first time, separated from my husband. The ache of solitude was palpable and tears flowed freely, an emotional tide that persisted until my children returned. Masking my sadness with a smile, I embraced the role of a resilient matriarch, determined to preserve the magic of Christmas for those I loved.

A Walk Through Shadows
Battling Bullying in School

The age-old spectre of bullying is a haunting wound woven through the fabric of human history. From playgrounds to boardrooms, the echoes of torment resonate across generations. As we strive for interventions, the question lingers – can we, in our flawed human nature, truly reshape this narrative?

One poignant facet of childhood bullying manifests in the plight of children changing schools. A seismic shift that, for many, becomes a gateway to isolation, estrangement and the persistent spectre of victimhood.

The evidence echoes through research[3], underscoring the vulnerability of those who, in search of a fresh start, often find themselves ensnared in the web of bullying once more.

I treaded the precarious path of relocation, uprooting my life during the summer of 1975. Unbeknownst to me, this shift marked the beginning of a tumultuous journey. Our new house, a proud fixture on a new estate, was a dormer bungalow standing testament to my mother's aspirations and perhaps even a hint of snobbery. The warmth of a coal fire exchanged for the meagre solace of a single gas flame, leaving our dwelling perpetually shrouded in winter's chill. Yet, the allure of a new bedroom and the proud presence of my Bontempi organ infused a spark of excitement.

The arrival of September heralded my initiation into a new school. Year Two unfolded in the confines of a well-established class, where existing bonds cast shadows on the arrival of an outsider. Uniforms, long socks failing in their duty, and the rhythmic scratch of an italic pen captured my unease.

However, the shadows of discomfort deepened further – the headteacher shared my surname, a curious coincidence that fuelled taunts. At the time, I didn't know that this shared name would become tinder for mocking whispers, branding me as kin to the headmistress. An unjust association that cast its long shadow over my early days in junior school.

My final year at junior school marked the onset of a dark chapter. The seemingly mundane act of walking home alone unravelled into a harrowing ordeal orchestrated by a high school bully, lurking around the graveyard entrance. Intimidation became a chilling routine, a solitary ordeal that I endured in silence. The fear, the anxiety and the physical aggression etched an indelible scar on my psyche.

The intervention of my mother, a ferocious advocate, unleashed a torrent of righteous anger that stopped the bully in her tracks. The school, recognising the urgency, adjusted its timings to ensure the safety of younger pupils. Yet, the scars lingered, and my transition to high school became a journey fraught with loneliness.

The confines of high school unleashed a fresh wave of adversity. The eccentricity of a teacher hurling board rubbers paled in comparison to the terror awaiting us by the hedge – an ominous barrier separating the younger students from the predatory older ones. Dodging the gauntlet of kicks and jeers became a daily ritual.

As I ventured into the second year of high school, hope flickered. But alas, the cruel twists of fate thrust me into the crosshairs of final-year tormentors. Their relentless campaign of name-calling and intimidation went unchecked until a distant relative intervened, banishing the shadows that clouded my high school days.

This, however, was not the end. The complexities of high school, and the intricate dance of acceptance, continued to elude me. The culmination of this tumultuous journey, my premature departure from high school, marked the reluctant conclusion of a chapter marred by the enduring scars of bullying.

The Key to Solitude
Navigating High School as a Latchkey Kid

The term 'latchkey child'[4] may date back to World War II, but its resonance persists in the echoes of today's afternoons, where thousands of older children navigate the solitude between 3 and 7 pm every weekday. In high school, my brother and I unwittingly joined the ranks of latchkey kids. With both parents fully immersed in their careers – Dad as a college lecturer and Mum as a seamstress at the Burberry sewing factory – our afternoons unfolded in a house shrouded in silence, devoid of a welcoming presence.

Mornings in our household bore the imprint of a rhythmic routine. Mum, the early riser, departed for work before the rest of us stirred, while Dad lingered in bed as we embarked on our day. This inconspicuous set-up worked to my advantage during my turbulent high school days, where my growing disdain for the institution prompted a new-found skill in the art of skiving – absenteeism without permission.

High school, particularly the third year, became a battleground of dislike. The period of choosing our school options surfaced, marking a pivotal juncture in our academic journey. The dichotomy of qualifications, be it GCSEs or CSEs, cast its shadow on our choices. A strict hierarchy dictated our paths, with the top stream confined to O levels. Being in the top stream meant taking O levels only, not a choice I wanted in maths due to the embedded memory of Mr Anderson writing in my report book, "Yvonne has let herself down again with her maths test." I went through my entire school life failing maths tests! If only I'd been allowed to take maths CSE, I would have at least come away with a qualification. Many years later, I persevered, retook the exam and at last got my maths qualification! This elitist structure, while limiting in academic terms, failed to stifle my subsequent achievements in the realm of work-based learning – a testament to the unpredictability of life's trajectory.

Options unfolded as a negotiation between student preference and parental veto, with Dad wielding the final say. In a divergence from my artistic aspirations, physics replaced art, leaving me with a curriculum that included English, literature, geography, music, computers, PE, physics and sex education. The latter two, my refuge for skiving, became a form of silent rebellion against a system that stifled my creative pursuits.

What started as a solitary act of absenteeism soon evolved into a collective endeavour with fellow rule-breakers. Astonishingly, the school refrained from reporting my truancy to my parents, a leniency that defied conventional expectations and certainly would not happen today. The cloak of invisibility extended to my physics class, where my absence went unnoticed, despite my name gracing the register!

One escapade stands out in my memory – a feigned journey to school, thwarted by an encounter with a friend outside the gates. A swift about-face led us back home, concealing ourselves behind the graveyard wall as Dad's car passed by, inadvertently granting me a reprieve from the consequences that loomed.

Guilt, a fleeting notion, remained elusive. I blamed my father for coercing me into the realm of physics. In retrospect, driven by the best of intentions, Dad grappled with the complexities of my educational choices.

Being a latchkey child meant returning home to an empty house, lacking the warmth and welcome one yearns for after a day at school. Central heating was a luxury we lacked, and the absence of a prepared meal left our house cold and desolate.

Mum was in hospital at one point, so a period of solitude unfolded, marked by unfamiliar responsibilities. I undertook the art of ironing, mastering the delicate chore of pressing Dad's daily shirts. Cooking, too, became a shared venture with Martin, guided by Nanna's wisdom in creating versatile meals from a single minced beef Bolognese.

Post-meals, the ritual of washing up became an unavoidable interruption to our childhood pursuits, sparking debates over roles and responsibilities in the clean-up process. The transition from outdoor play to indoor chores bore the imprint of sibling contention, a dance repeated with each passing evening in the life of a latchkey kid.

Summary

As children, we wish our childhoods away – not deliberately; we just want to grow up and be seen as mature. The passage of school hastens our wants to go to the next level, as no sooner are we leaving nursery than we are told we are going to big school. When we get to 12, we want to be a teenager. However, when you leave school, whether to go into higher education or to join the world of work, it is then that you realise childhood is fleeting. As one gets older, childhood and school days are often tinged with nostalgic memories, the what-ifs and different paths taken.

Yvonne's Top Tips

- Don't wish your children's childhood away for them; let them develop in their own time. One day, you will blink and that childhood will be gone.

- Think about what you give the child or children in your life – remember, they'd rather have your time than money.

- Make memories that last for both you and the child in your life.

- Think about how different your holidays would be if you weren't all tethered to the mobile phone; God forbid that you would have to talk to each other! Try sitting around the table, get the cards out or a game of Monopoly, as you and everyone involved will remember those moments.

Memory Box 2:
A Life-Changing Moment

Shattered Bonds

In the swirling chaos of adolescence, my teenage years unfolded as a series of rebellions against the constrictions of my father's expectations. The disappointing clutches of a physics class held me captive, a realm far removed from the vibrant strokes of an art class that had beckoned my spirit. In the 1980s, societal norms dictated that girls shouldn't delve into 'boys' subjects.' Yet, in that classroom, I sat as one of only four girls in a sea of equations and rigid formulas.

My desire to wield a paintbrush instead of grappling with the laws of physics clashed with my father's wishes. A college lecturer in engineering, he believed I should follow in his footsteps. The clash of generations manifested as an unspoken power play. In those times, children were still navigating the transition from being 'seen and not heard' to asserting their voices, and, beneath my compliant exterior, I harboured a stubborn determination to shape my destiny.

Paradoxically, my father, who was a skilled artist and musician, dismissed art as an unworthy pursuit for his daughter. It became clear that his aspirations for me were not rooted in my dreams, but his unfulfilled desires. The realisation struck me like a lightning bolt: he was sculpting my future without consulting the artist within me!

Every disagreement with my father became a battleground for independence during those turbulent teenage years. The rebellious spirit within me led to silent battles where I learned to dig my heels in, a precursor to the mantra, "It's my way or the highway." Physics classes became my silent protest, a choice I now recognise as regrettable. Looking back, I realise the missed opportunity to engage young minds in education. The teenage thirst for excitement and adventure is often drowned in the monotony of uninspiring lessons. I regret not delving into physics, but it was never presented in a way that ignited my curiosity.

As the neon glow of the early 1980s cast its glare over my teenage rebellion, the cultural landscape was shifting beneath our feet. It was an era dominated by big hair, synthesisers, and societal norms were beginning to crack. The music of the time, pulsating with the beats of bands like Duran Duran and Madonna, served as the anthem for our generation's desire for autonomy and individuality.

The park was our clandestine haven, and echoed with the laughter and camaraderie of girls navigating the uncharted waters of adolescence. It was a space where childhood innocence shed its skin, revealing the complexities of burgeoning womanhood. Amid the rustle of windblown leaves and the distant hum of city life, we shared our dreams, fears and secrets that tethered us together.

With its bold fashion and experimental spirit, the 1980s mirrored the internal struggles of a generation caught between tradition and a burgeoning desire for self-expression. The air crackled with the excitement of change, but within the confines of my home, tradition held a tenacious grip. My father, a product of a different era, clung to conservative ideals, unknowingly stifling the artistic aspirations that ran through my veins.

As I grappled with the tug-of-war between tradition and rebellion, the theme of parental disconnect loomed large. My parents, seemingly caught in the undertow of their own lives, failed to notice the subtle shifts in my demeanour. Once resilient and independent, the latchkey child morphed into a teenager cloaked in defiance, seeking refuge in the anonymity of the park's shadows.

The park, a microcosm of societal dynamics, witnessed the evolving understanding of relationships. In the early eighties, conversations about sexuality and diversity were still whispers drowned out by the louder voices of conformity. Unaware of the broader spectrum of human experiences, our group of friends navigated the uncharted waters of teenage attraction and the mysteries of adulthood.

Amid this cultural whirlwind, my path took an unexpected and life-changing turn. The themes of rebellion, parental disconnect and societal transformation converged in a crescendo that would redefine the trajectory of my life. The neon-lit nights of the eighties would soon give way to the harsh realities of adulthood, but not before the echoes of that rebellious era resonated through the corridors of memory, shaping the chapters yet to unfold in life.

Teenagers are a force of rebellion, questioning authority and seeking their path. Amid my academic standoff, a storm of hormonal changes and the assertion of authority marked my journey into adulthood. At the same time, my life felt like a tempest; decisions imposed on me intensified the isolation, as if my parents were oblivious to the tempest within.

I morphed into a teenager exploiting freedom. As my friends sought permission to explore the world, I surrendered to the belief that asking for permission was an exercise in futility. The responsibility of caring for my younger brother during my parents' pub visits became an escape strategy. With Martin sworn to secrecy, I seized the opportunity to venture into the park, leaving him and the confines of home behind.

Hanging out in the park symbolised freedom, a sanctuary where conversations flowed uninhibited by adult judgement. It was a haven where 13-year-old me explored choices without the weight of consequences. The park was my 'place' for self-discovery, where my voice echoed in the company of like-minded friends.

My parents, seemingly oblivious to the perils of teenage hangouts, never warned me about the vulnerabilities we faced. The eighties shielded us from discussions about homosexuality and gender biases. The fair that swept into town brought the echoes of cautionary tales. My father's warning about travelling fair folk seeking to steal pretty girls took root in my adolescent imagination. Little did I realise that the theft was happening within the confines of our familial bonds as the threads connecting parent and child began to fray. Despite my father's strict discipline, my careless rebellion whispered, "What he doesn't know won't hurt him."

I had no idea that these seemingly carefree days in the park would become the backdrop for a more profound rebellion – one that would shatter the bonds between parent and child, propelling me into the tumultuous terrain of unexpected motherhood.

The park served as an escape for me and my friends. We relished the sense of power that came with skipping school and venturing out into the world on our own terms. Spending more time in the park taught us the importance of decision-making, even though some choices were unwise and consequences were not always considered.

One day, whilst sitting with friends on a bench overlooking the swings, we noticed the leaves and branches of the dense bushes edging the area moving in an odd way in the wind. We glanced at each other, curious. We noticed a shadowy figure lurking within the bushes, and we continued to stare, transfixed.

Suddenly, a man stepped out from behind the bushes, baring his penis for all to see. We were shocked and startled, but we couldn't seem to look away from the perversion unfolding before us.

We quickly headed back to school to report our disturbing experience, and as we sat with the teacher and tried to recount what had happened, one of the girls blurted out, "He stood there waggling it." Her crass choice of words pained me, but we couldn't help but giggle in nervous shock. After that incident, many people avoided the park altogether, but my friends and I were far from deterred.

Growing older, my body began to change and I became aware of the attention boys would give me. Hanging out with groups of boys a little older than us due to their involvement in rugby, we enjoyed flirting and chatting about our shared interests – our favourite subject being boys, of course! Before long, I started meeting confident boys outside our usual park meet-ups. Keeping these secret dates from my parents fuelled my impulsive behaviour.

Without the ease of mobile phones or a telephone in our home, the only way to secure plans was to do so at school or while we were out together. My parents had no idea where I was, and as previously mentioned, Martin was sworn to secrecy. The more daring we became in our escapades, the more reckless I became. Drinking cider in the park was a regular occurrence, and my frequent absences from school went largely unnoticed by my parents.

One particularly hazy evening, a group of boys and girls returned to my house while my parents were out. I drank too much and eventually fell asleep in my bed. Later, my best friend would tell me that she had stopped one of the boys from what she called 'interfering' with me while I was sleeping. This should have been a wake-up call for me to consider the risks of my impulsive behaviour, but at the time, I ignored any warning signs and continued down a dangerous path.

Like most teenage girls, my perceived emotional maturity made me feel fully equipped to handle sexual relationships. The truth, however, was that I acted purely on impulse without considering the possible consequences of my actions. Ultimately, this was a lesson that would stay with me for a long time to come.

Navigating Teen Pregnancy in the 1980s
A Tapestry of Challenges

One night, whilst lying in bed, I had the strangest feeling in my stomach. It felt as though something within me had shifted. A disquieting awareness gnawed at me, something foreign to my usual carefree demeanour. Something didn't feel right, but I did not know what.

I soon realised how it felt to be worried about something, and up until that moment, it had not been part of my makeup. It was an alien feeling to me and I was struggling to hold it together.

That night, as usual, Mum and Dad were at the pub, but this particular night, I was still awake when they returned home. Mum always came into our bedrooms to check on us when she came home.

As soon as she entered my room, the tears rolled down my cheeks.

Naivety slapped me across the face with a jolt. Here I was, with no sex education, and not understanding the need for protection. It dawned on me that I must be pregnant. After all, I knew what I had done, but I thought I was untouchable and that becoming pregnant happened to other girls, not me!

I blurted out, "Mum, I think I'm pregnant!"

She turned to me and said, "Don't worry; we will sort it out with a visit to the doctor."

My dad wasn't told anything, so we went to see the doctor; he knew everyone in the family and had once lived next door to Nanna and Grandad. He examined me and took a urine sample to send off for confirmation. There were no home pregnancy testing kits in the eighties. He told both me and Mum that he didn't think I was pregnant. What a relief...

When people say they don't believe someone doesn't know that they are pregnant, you should listen to them without judgement. I was 30 weeks pregnant before the realisation set in. I was a 15-year-old schoolgirl; I'd had no form of morning sickness, I'd never taken any notice of my periods, and I had no noticeable increase in weight.

A week later, we went back for the results. It was confirmed that I was over 30 weeks pregnant and was "too far gone" to have a termination so I would have to go through with it. Mum and I were in shock; she was the one who broke the news to Dad whilst I waited outside, scared of his reaction. I don't remember Dad's response, but he went to the pub.

It's strange how you remember some things whilst blocking out others. I remember that evening as if it were yesterday: Dad at the pub, Mum in the kitchen, my friend came around, and we talked about having a cot in my bedroom and bringing the baby up at home. That was the last conversation I had about how I would look after my baby.

My parents removed me from school and sent me to my aunty's every day. As they were working, they couldn't look after me during the day. My aunty was also pregnant so she became my weekday carer. I always felt that I had disgraced the family as social services had to be involved. A designated social worker visited on Friday afternoons as Mum only worked until lunch and Dad didn't have lessons to teach, so, in principle, we would all be at home.

Like clockwork, the social worker would turn up on a Friday afternoon. There was always a vacant chair as my dad was undoubtedly at the pub, and these emotional visits and conversations were outside his comfort zone. So, I would update the social worker, answer a few questions, and then she'd be gone in what felt like less than half an hour!

I only ever saw one friend during the remainder of my pregnancy. When it got out that I was pregnant, Martin had a fight to protect my name. I was now known as a "slag". I had made mistakes, but so had lots of other girls, the difference being they'd 'got away with it', and I'd been caught.

I had no idea when the decision was made that I would not keep the baby and that he/she would be put up for adoption by strangers. I remember listening to Mum and Dad's conversations on an evening after the pub's closing hours. One particular discussion looms large in my mind; the daughter of a close friend of Dad's had a baby, and he told Dad, "Do not change the decision of having the baby adopted, as it will ruin your daughter's life."

I don't think I truly understood what adoption meant, but I lacked the understanding or ability to question decisions made on my behalf.

A Silent Birth, an Unspoken Goodbye

Like all pregnant mothers, I found myself navigating the routine of hospital visits. This ritual connects the threads of expectation and anxiety that weave through the thoughts of impending motherhood. Unaware and unprepared, without participating in any prenatal classes, the mystique of childbirth remained a mystery to me.

February 4th 1983 marked the beginning of a journey that, unbeknownst to me, would carve itself into the depths of my memory. I was in labour, a force of nature that respects no schedule. As fate would have it, my father was at the pub when the first contractions seized me. Panic ensued and the ambulance became my lifeline. My mother, who couldn't drive, was my companion, by my side in the ambulance, a comforting presence in the storm that was about to unfold.

The hospital room I was ushered into remains furrowed in my mind with crystal clarity, a clinical white space with a bed strategically placed at its heart. Monitors flanked the bed, soon to be my constant companions, documenting the rhythm of my contractions. The door to a small toilet occupied one corner and a window to the world stood beside it, though my view remained obscured by the intensity of the moment.

The medical procedures were both necessary and uncomfortable, and as I grappled with the challenges of an enema during contractions, I sensed the impending arrival of a new life. Seven hours passed in the blink of an eye, and my firstborn son came into the world on the morning of the following day, 5th February 1983. My mother stood by my side, a pillar of support in the whirlwind of emotions that enveloped me.

But I now recognise what happened next as a cruel twist of fate. My son, my precious baby boy, was swiftly taken from the room, cradled in the arms of a nurse. I never saw him, never held him. Emotionless, I watched as the door closed behind them, leaving me in a void of uncertainty and unspoken grief.

Penning these words now, tears well in my eyes, for the pain of that moment is as vivid now as it was then. In the room's silence, no words or conversations were exchanged. The hospital staff moved me to a side room in the maternity ward, where the cries of other babies served as a haunting reminder of what I had lost. Nobody even asked me if I wanted to see or hold my son; they had made the decision – he was to be adopted.

After leaving the hospital, I still had to register and name my baby. Life moved forward, but the ache of the unknown lingered. I had no idea where he had gone, what he would be told, or what name he would carry in his new life.

My education became a secondary concern, and a petite lady on a moped arrived at my doorstep to home-school me and provide whatever support she could. Yet, she didn't have the expertise for any of the subjects that I was taking! And so, life unfolded, leaving me with a void that time could not fill and unanswered questions.

Navigating Shadows, Building Bridges

Returning to school after the birth of my son felt like stepping into a world that had moved on without me. The exam hall, once a familiar battleground, now echoed with the whispers of unfamiliar faces. I sat among my peers, but the sense of being an outsider looking in lingered like a quiet ghost in the corner of the room. Despite the dissonance, I emerged with qualifications, a testament to resilience in the face of personal turmoil.

Yet, the haunting thought of untapped potential lingered like a soft ache.

As unpredictable as the winds sweeping through the Yorkshire landscape, life's path offered me unexpected twists. In pursuing purpose and progress, I worked tirelessly, engaging in night classes and embracing further education to propel my career forward. The classrooms became my sanctuary, each lesson a step towards reclaiming the dreams that motherhood had momentarily eclipsed. In true Northern style, I pressed on, determined to shape a destiny of my own making.

As an adult and still curious, a seemingly innocuous request for my social services records unveiled a Pandora's box of revelations. The reports penned by social workers painted a stark picture – one where decisions that shaped my life were made by others, not by the one living that life. The ink on those pages bore witness to a failure in protection, a system that faltered in safeguarding the very soul it was meant to nurture.

Within those lines on the page, the words of a social worker echoed with painful clarity. Her concerns were voiced about the profound impact that the adoption of my baby would have on my future self. She offered a visionary understanding of the scars that would linger, but, like an unanswered plea in the wind, nothing was done to assuage her concerns. The echoes of unheeded warnings reverberate through the corridors of time, a testament to the silent battles fought and lost in the bureaucratic labyrinth.

With its intricate threads of joy and sorrow, life continued to unfurl. Each revelation became a stepping stone, a reminder that the ink of social worker reports did not solely dictate the narrative of my life. It was a story of resilience, forging ahead against the current and reclaiming my destiny.

Summary

There are times in our lives when we do things that can change our path. As teenagers, we don't know what this path looks like, we have no idea of our destination, and can only be led by those around us. I felt like I was a disappointment to those around me. My childhood innocence was gone. As parents, we cocoon our children away from the harsh reality of life, but we need to be mindful that we also give them the tools to live in today's ever-changing world.

Yvonne's Top Tips

- Think about things that have happened to you that you can share with the young people in your life to keep them safe.

- Don't beat yourself up about something you did; remember, everyone makes mistakes.

- Respect yourself and teach others to do the same – make a note of how you can do this, and what support you need, then reach out.

Memory Box 3:
Motherly Love

This description of motherly love is mine. Yours might be different. It is also important to note that not all mothers feel this love instantly. While I paint this picture of motherly love, you will discover I have also endured great pain in pregnancy and childbirth.

Imagine a sky filled with cascading rainbow colours as rockets explode, shedding twinkling sparks and lighting up the darkness. It feels like a fountain of expansive emotion fizzing and popping from within, enveloping a love beyond all others. The awe and wonder of that moment when you hold your baby for the first long-awaited time in your arms encompasses all that is sacred and magical about life. A new life full of hope, joy, love and wonder. A love that bonds a mother and her baby forever.

As a mother, I believe that when you hold the innocence of humankind in your arms for the first time, the pain of delivering this new life into the world melts away. It is the elixir of all painkillers; the mind is a beautiful thing that blots out the pain and forgets it in an instant!

When you tenderly cast your eyes on your baby, everything seems right with the world. Here is the little miracle you created, and whether covered in blood or the white creamy biofilm (vernix caseosa), you instantly fall in love, a love beyond measure. You count the fingers and toes, scan the length of your baby, and express an enormous sigh of relief that all is well.

After that first rush of adrenaline, you realise that this bundle of joy relies on you for everything, but that is okay because you would give your life to protect your child. You look at your baby, and their eyes may be closed but that is okay, because you infuse them with unconditional love that will return to you as they grow.

There is magic in holding the innocence of your newborn baby, knowing that no one can ever take away that all-consuming feeling of motherly love. It is your moment to cherish and look back on when you need a boost in life.

My first pregnancy and birth were not as described above. Being a teenager of 15 was not the ideal time to become pregnant. As mentioned in *Memory Box 2*, I didn't even know I was pregnant until around 30 weeks. There was no immediate joy, but as it sank in, I allowed myself to dream about life with my baby, only to discover that the illusion would soon be shattered.

As you can imagine, my parents had a different story to tell. They had another outcome for me and my baby. I do not blame them because they believed they were protecting me from a life of struggle and imprisonment at such a tender age and stage in life. They decided to have my baby adopted. Words were spoken to me and I was offered no choice. There was an unspoken understanding that as soon as the baby was born, cruelly, it would be snatched away, never to be seen by me again. This is exactly what happened.

As mentioned in *Memory Box 2*, I gave birth with my mother at my side. There were no fireworks for me, only sadness. I could not and did not feel the joy of giving birth to my son, and was not even allowed to hold my innocent bundle of love and happiness in my arms. It is incredible how the human brain can protect you from emotional pain. It blotted out this whole experience, but one cannot suppress such a momentous occasion without an eruption of emotion emerging at some point, and one never knows when that time will come. It was a cold and mindless act that would haunt me later in life.

◊◊◊◊◊

After the birth, I was isolated, adding to the turmoil and pain I had endured and the continued torment buried deep within. No one asked me what I wanted, but the expectation was to pick up where I left off, studying for my exams. In true old British fashion of adopting a 'stiff upper lip,' life moved on. I returned to school, taking my exams alongside a sea of faces oblivious to the turmoil brewing beneath my surface. The once lively friendships, now mere shadows of the past, seemed like distant threads in the corridors of my memory. The camaraderie I once cherished had melted, leaving me feeling like an outsider in my own world.

Looking back, I was a warrior, bravely facing my battles in the secrecy of my soul, my emotions a storm, raging against the conformity demanded by society. A girl robbed of her innocence and thrust into motherhood, interrupting her dreams and love of life, yet expected to carry on as if I had simply skinned my knee.

On 5th February 1984, whilst at college, I broke down into tears. It was my son's first birthday. I had not forgotten, nor did I every year after. I would cry alone, then lock the memory back in its box.

Time marched on, and the memories of youth, a time of boundless freedom and innocence, were also locked away in my Memory Box.

Like my peers, I embarked on a journey that seemed destined for adventure. Love wrapped its arms around me, convincing my heart that Rob was my one true love. We were young, but our dreams were endless.

With jobs in hand, we explored the world of adulthood, ready to pave a path uniquely ours. We transformed a house into a haven filled with our dreams and aspirations. In those moments, I felt the weight of adulthood on my shoulders, yet it was exhilarating. Looking back, those were the days of blissful naivety and the joy of forging our destiny.

A spark of joy ignited my soul as I received the most precious gift – the news that I was pregnant! Everything around me seemed to shimmer with a new radiance, for this was no ordinary discovery; it was a symphony of emotions, a kaleidoscope of sensations unlike anything I had experienced before.

The excitement coursed through my veins and was nothing short of magical – a "wow" factor that left me breathless. My life transformed at that moment; I was standing at the crossroads of love and happiness, immersed in a developing relationship, and now, on the cusp of motherhood again. Our hearts filled with delight as we now lovingly renovated our second home, cherishing every moment of this perfect chapter in our lives.

Like young dreamers, we had talked about starting a family, yet the prospect of a baby seemed thrilling and daunting. Amid the uncertainties, my heart overflowed with unbridled ecstasy. Oh, my goodness, life was growing inside me, an awe-inspiring miracle unfolding in the sanctuary of my womb. I cradled the secret, whispering to my unborn child, "You are my baby, and I will protect you with every fibre of my being!"

I embraced the power of choice at this moment, for this time the journey was **MINE** to navigate. **No one** could dictate my future; it was mine to shape and mould. And as I held on to the reins of my destiny, a sense of empowerment washed over me like a warm, comforting tide. With every beat of my heart and breath, I embraced the wonder of my pregnancy with an unyielding spirit. I was the guardian of this tiny life within, and I vowed to nurture it with all the love and strength within me. This was my baby, and the journey of motherhood had begun, a passage where I would savour every moment, cherish every flutter, and hold the key to unlocking the boundless love that awaited us both.

And so, I walked this pregnant path with unwavering determination and an open heart, knowing that this baby and I were embarking on a journey filled with love, hope and the promise of an everlasting bond. With each passing day, I marvelled at the miracle of life and felt profound gratitude for the privilege of being a vessel of love and life itself.

Life, a relentless teacher, revealed its cruel hand as my joy swiftly switched into sorrow, and my heartache knew no bounds when faced with the devastating reality of a miscarriage. In the depths of my grief, an avalanche of thoughts swirled within my mind, each whispering that this was a punishment, a cosmic retribution for the difficult decision I had made in the past – the relinquishment of my firstborn child.

Dealing with the inner turmoil, the agony that gnawed at my soul became an arduous journey fraught with guilt, hopelessness and an overwhelming sense of being punished. It was as though I was trapped in a labyrinth of despair, where darkness loomed and the light of hope seemed ever distant. In the 1990s, mental health care was a distant concept, and seeking solace by sharing my emotional turmoil with another person was a distant dream.

In the stillness of those times, I discovered an inner, meaningful strength. Even in the face of adversity, I held on to hope, believing that the sun would pierce through the clouds one day and a new dawn of healing would rise. But for now, I clung to the flicker of resilience, for it was all I had, a beacon of light amid a storm that raged within.

I didn't tell anybody how I felt because I was also dealing with my husband's pain. The thoughts in my head tried to reassure me that it wasn't his fault. He was losing his first child, and I was losing my second child because I didn't get to keep my first. My brain was in overdrive, throwing all sorts of reasoning for me to decipher and try to come to terms with. Why is life overcomplicated? Your mind whizzes with spurious things that shouldn't be there. With no counselling, it was back to that Northern way of thinking: "Okay, you've had a rough ride; now get on with it."

Even though I came to terms with the miscarriage and tried to quieten the raucous thoughts, I struggled to understand why. After all, I fell pregnant so quickly the first time. A few weeks after the miscarriage, I went for a smear test. I think it might have been routine after miscarrying. The smear test revealed some abnormal cells, resulting in a period of treatment. I now believe the miscarriage was a blessing in disguise because a delay in discovering my abnormal cells, or even not discovering them at all, would have meant a totally different outcome.

I became numb to everything that was happening to me. It seemed as if I was going from one crisis to the next, all health-related. I was relieved that cancer had not taken hold of me. Nevertheless, I had to endure the treatment. How long was it going to take?

How often did I have to go to Pontefract Hospital, put my legs in those stirrups, and look at the ceiling? I was scared and could smell the skin burning as the doctor removed the abnormal cells. The one distraction I had was looking up at the ceiling. Picture the scene – you are lying on a hospital bed, legs in stirrups, everyone looking at the most private parts of your body, and on the ceiling is a poster. Not just any poster, but caricatures of couples on the ski slopes having sex in different positions... To say I was surprised is an understatement! Did it take my mind off the invasive procedure? Yes, it did!

Despite all that I had been through since the age of 15, I was grateful to be alive and to survive two pregnancies without a baby to hold as well as a cancer scare.

The sun finally shone on me not long after my miscarriage when I discovered I was pregnant again. This time, there is a happy ending, and that picture I painted at the start of this Memory Box was my experience at the birth of my daughter. Nothing and no one can ever take that away from me. Remember to hold onto your bright and joyful experiences because nothing life or people can throw at you will ever take them away. It is yours to treasure to your last breath. I beg you not to lock it away, but to take it out of the Memory Box and feel those feelings now and then to motivate you in darker times. Those experiences are there for a reason, and we should always revisit the joy they bring.

Rob and I married not long after the miscarriage. Our marriage blessed us with three daughters, so life has lessons to teach us and provides situations and circumstances to experience the whole spectrum of emotions. I have learned to embrace them because I will become stronger and develop resilience that allows me to bounce back, no matter what.

Life with my three girls was great. I was experiencing the whole gambit of joy, love and challenge that having a young family brings – having my third daughter meant that I had three children under four – but I would not change anything for the world. I was in my happy place.

Motherly love evolves and grows as you travel through life, from the explosion of love when you hold your baby in your arms for the first time, to all of the trials and tribulations of watching, guiding and nurturing the child or children in your life as they grow. The power of love is incredible – and the more you love, the more love you feel, and the more love you have to give. It makes me think of my grandparents, who had endless children and grandchildren, yet managed to show love to each and every one of them.

Have you ever thought about how you love the child/ children in your life? Undoubtedly you love them very much, but you have different ways of showing it, depending upon their personalities. For instance, some children love cuddles, while others do not.

I want to share with you my motherly love story about each of my three daughters. I will begin with my youngest daughter's birth.

Picture me, back in the hospital for the birth of my third (fifth) child and I can only describe it as a *Tom and Jerry*[1] cartoon! If you know or remember those cartoons, there was a big friendly maid who was always jolly and laughing, but terrified of Jerry the mouse; every time he appeared, she would jump up on to a tottering three-legged stool.

My midwife reminds me of this character; friendly and always laughing. She is in the room with me. Here I am on the bed, enduring the pain of labour and childbirth. I'm crushing Rob's hand while I'm floating up to the ceiling on the gas and air, and I do not want to come down! My jolly midwife is trying to coax me down, and I am nearing the point of pushing and bearing down. No matter what she says, I refuse to give up my gas and air.

She asks, "Would you like to see your baby being born?"

Replying in gas-and-air stupor, "Yeah, I'd love to see my baby being born. But how do you do that?"

At that moment, she fetches a long, full-length mirror and places it at the bottom of the bed, where I witness my baby being born. At last, I understand why I need to push, pant or do anything else I need to do. It is the most fantastic birth of all my children because I witness her entering the world.

After holding my baby, a second midwife took her away to be measured and weighed.

I told my jolly midwife, "She will weigh 7lb 10oz."

"How did you know?"

"Because her two sisters were the same weight!"

She laughed with sheer joy, hearty warmth and kindness. I was right – Jade weighed 7lb 10oz, exactly the same as her two sisters!

I was so in love with my new daughter. My motherly love only wanted the best for my baby as all parents do.

As you watch your child grow, you want the best for them. Your love evolves and responds to their personalities. By the time Jade reached 17, her understanding of her sexuality was clear. She found the courage to reveal she was bisexual. Now she could get on with being herself. We always loved and accepted her for who she was and understood her boyish traits growing up, revealing an acceptance of her identity.

Emma

My first daughter, Emma, has a strong personality. She had ginger curly hair, and her character lived up to the idea of a redhead's feisty nature. Being the firstborn (in this family unit), she was the boss, especially with her sisters. Whatever Emma said, went. You may remember the children's programme, *Rugrats*[2]? Emma was nicknamed after the character Angelica who was bossy and always got what she wanted! (My dad had the joy of nicknaming all of my girls!) Emma would always mother and boss her sisters around, but they never seemed to mind. They followed her every move and did whatever she told them; they idolised her. Even today, Emma continues to take the lead, and what she says still goes. There are only 18 months between each of the girls. From an early age, she led the way and set an example.

When my girls were small, for many a year, my in-laws often took them to Cleethorpes during the summer holidays, where they had a caravan. We were always grateful because it would help us and give us some breathing space, as raising a family is hard work and tiring.

Emma was constantly pushing the boundaries. On many occasions, we would say, "If you don't do X, then you won't get Y." Sometimes when she was still young enough, we would say, "Santa's watching, so you need to be a good girl or he won't bring you presents!" You often ask yourself, "At what point do I put my foot down?" Motherly love never leaves you, but children test your patience and authority to establish healthy relationships with them while setting boundaries. After all, you only want to keep them safe, whatever 'safe' is for you.

On one occasion, the girls were going to accompany Grandma and Grandad (Rob's parents) to the caravan for a short break. Emma was being difficult so we threatened not to allow her to go. But, as per many occasions, she did not believe we would see it through, so she pushed her luck and broke the boundary once again. We informed her that she would not go with her sisters to the caravan with Grandma and Grandad. It was tough, but we stuck to our guns.

The other two girls left for the caravan and we all knew they would have a lovely time. Emma was cross and sulked at home. We intended to teach her a lesson but were then going to surprise her by driving her down to join her siblings after a couple of days. We didn't want her to entirely miss out on this precious time with her sisters and grandparents.

Emma had just started high school and, like many young people, she was finding her feet at this transitional stage of her life. On the day the other two left, she sat around sulking, thinking deeply about the consequences.

We had a little kid's motorbike that belonged to Jade. Emma pleaded with us to be allowed to play with it outside and so we succumbed to her demands. We much preferred her playing on that, as opposed to the petrol scooter that belonged to one of the boys she played with. We believed the little motorbike to be more stable and therefore safer.

The next day, some of her friends came calling for her. At this stage, we were softening and decided she could go out to play with her friends and the motorbike. We had a paddock and our house was on a single-track lane in the middle of the countryside so there was no traffic, except the occasional tractor. It was an accessible and safe space for kids to play.

Emma was warned in no uncertain terms not to go on the petrol scooter but to keep to her motorbike. Off they went to do what young people do, have fun…

About an hour later, I could hear a boy shouting and getting louder and louder.

"Mrs Tomlinson! Mrs Tomlinson!"

He came sprinting towards me to alert me that something had happened to Emma. All he could say was, "We're sorry, we're sorry!"

"Why, what's happened?" I gasped.

Emma was in the distance; there was blood everywhere. Her chin looked like it was hanging off her face, her elbows were scraped, and she had grazed her knees. It soon transpired that, of course, she had swapped the motorbike for the petrol scooter. Typical! You tell a child not to do something, yet they try it anyway because they believe they are invincible. The small wheels of the scooter going over a large stone unbalanced Emma, throwing her onto the gravel of the country lane, resulting in terrible skin abrasions.

We went straight to A&E. Emma was quietly sobbing and was in great pain, but I was a total mess! I was so concerned that my girl was going to be disfigured and that her wounds would become infected due to the specs of gravel and dirt from the track. Emma was strong – perhaps it was the shock that kept her calm.

As they injected her chin to numb it so they could clean it up, the blood drained from my head. I'm looking at my baby, and then becoming all woozy and having to be supported so as not to pass out! How embarrassing!

The medical staff cleaned Emma up and we brought her home. The very next day, we drove her down to the caravan. We felt terrible about the whole incident. Even though she hadn't listened to us, we felt so guilty, as we had kept her back from the holiday. If she'd gone down with her sisters as she was initially meant to, she wouldn't have had the accident…

Her wounds started to heal, and even now, she is still proud of her 'war wounds' from that childhood accident. She has scars on her chin and knee, and is immensely proud of the one on her knee because it looks like a Nike tick!

Life constantly transitions. You are often reminded of a stage your child went through when they are experiencing something new. I remember Emma going off to university, but for me it was precisely like taking her to school for her first day. I cried, as did many other mothers (some more than the child!), on Emma's first day of school as this is huge milestone in a child's life.

As a parent or carer, it is about letting go as the child becomes more independent. They are beginning to think for themselves, make choices, make friends and learn to be themselves. It's the same when they move from primary school to high school. Each is a milestone and a transition into a new period of their life and a step closer to independence, although, at the time, you do not see it like that.

Hindsight and wisdom are great healers and give you a knowing and acceptance that all is well in the passage of life and time.

It was no surprise that I cried again when Emma went to university, worrying about her living alone away from home for the first time. Deep down, I knew she would be fine, confident that we had given her the tools to be independent and make good choices. Whether her intentions were good or bad, we were always there to support her. I also knew she had outgrown her siblings; it was time for a fledgling to leave the nest. She needed her space and time to be herself and establish herself in whatever way she chose.

She wanted to do a teacher training degree, but we felt there was a lot more opportunity if she chose a business management degree. However, she was adamant she wanted to teach. Naturally, we supported her choice because her life and happiness are meaningful. Getting back in the car, turning on the ignition and driving off was a mixture of both sadness and joy. It is an absolute yin and yang moment, because you realise your baby has grown. It hits you like a ton of bricks and is yet another roller coaster in your journey as a parent, yet another severing of the umbilical cord. However, no matter what, your motherly love keeps strengthening and giving in such an unconditional way to your child.

When life throws you lemons, make lemonade. That's precisely what happened to Emma. She realised university was financially challenging and was determined to complete her degree, but had to find a different way to do it in her second year so she could save money. Paying for university accommodation five days a week meant less money in her pocket. Money seemed to be a driver for her at this stage and she knew she could work at the local golf club at home and earn some money, so she moved back home with us in her second and third year.

As we lived in the country, all three girls were encouraged to drive as soon as they reached the age of 17. We bought their first cars and paid for the upkeep in the first year and then they had to fund the running costs themselves. We gave them some initial help, but wanted them to become financially independent.

Emma loved driving to Scarborough for her degree and returning home where she didn't have to pay as we did not charge her rent. Financially, she came out of university in a good place – much better than most students who have just finished their degree. She now had money in the bank and was able to upgrade her car. We felt that supporting Emma in her choices was the right thing to do. I know that everything I instilled in her as a mother was positive.

After graduating with a teaching degree, Emma changed direction and went into recruitment instead. But then she decided to go into nursery management, so still had that educational pull. Like many others, Covid gave her another opportunity to stay at home with her children now that she is a mother too. She continues to make good choices and loves the independence it gives her.

That is all a mother wants for her child; to be loved, to be happy, to be content.

Amy

When Amy was born, she had white hair, about an inch long. It was so endearing and beautiful as it stood on end. It was a talking point and she managed to keep her mop of blonde hair, rather than it falling out as the first baby hair often does. Every time she moved, it reminded me of a dandelion swaying in the gentle summer breeze. It was so cute!

Amy was the opposite of Emma in both personality and style. Amy loved dolls, but Emma 'didn't do dolls', so there was no way Emma would have anything to do with them. From the beginning, Amy was a girly girl liking all the once stereotypical girl stuff. As she became a toddler, she had a little blonde ponytail that reminded me of baby Pebbles in the TV show, *The Flintstones*[3]!

True to our family tradition, Amy was given a nickname by my dad – 'Amy Wibwob'. I don't know where he got the name from, but she loved it when she was tiny. However, as she grew older, she fell out of love with it so became 'Fluffy' instead, because we always believed she had her head in the clouds, in her own world.

As a teenager, she changed and hit puberty early. She became well-developed in what seemed like overnight! We had arguments over her wearing a bra. She didn't want to wear one, but was developing fast and a T-shirt wasn't adequate. I would say, "You need to cover yourself up and wear a bra!" We had a huge standoff in the car one day. I was adamant I wasn't taking her anywhere until she went back inside and put a bra on, but she was being stubborn so sat in the car, and wouldn't get out! It's pretty funny now, but it was such a headache then. It's about knowing what to fight over and when to stand firm.

My little princess was growing up and changing quite dramatically. Amy was the one causing us sleepless nights. As soon as her friends called, off she went into the night, ignoring the curfews we set and staying out late, drinking with her friends. There were several nights we didn't even know where she was, so Rob would go out looking for her while I stayed with Emma and Jade, who were fast asleep. When your child is out in the night all alone and you don't know where they are, or if they are safe, your motherly love kicks in. That protective, nurturing side of you raises its head.

In front of me, this little princess had metamorphised into a rebel. A people-pleaser she was not, but finding her own two feet, her identity and her place in the world. Of course, this is precisely as it should be, the road to independence. But it can be tough to deal with.

Amy is a daddy's girl – always was and always will be, and her sisters know this. Even today, if there any disputes in the family, her sisters tease her, saying that she will always back him up and take his side. As a mother, watching that father-and-daughter relationship bloom into something solid and beautiful is quite endearing.

When it was Amy's turn to leave the nest, things were different. It was a time when my marriage was sadly failing and I decided to leave the family home. These added challenges brought Amy a lot of grief. She thought we would split up if she went to university, so felt that if she stayed at home that meant we wouldn't split up.

As a mother, this is a hard pill to swallow. You do not want to add to your child's misery, but at the same time, you cannot remain miserable yourself. The analogy that springs to mind is putting on your own oxygen mask first before you help anyone else. I had to be strong, happy and healthy to give my girls the best.

I had many conversations with Amy about her desire to go to university to study teaching; like her sister, she had worked extremely hard to get the results she needed. I reassured her that whatever was happening between her father and me didn't need to impact what she needed to do for her future. The emotional roller coaster we were on heightened my sadness that Amy was going to university. Still, I knew it was the right decision for her because she didn't need to be part of what was happening to myself and Rob at home.

A marriage break-up is a difficult time for everyone involved. Amy was struggling with the divorce and her decision to go to university, and there was great tension between the two of us. There were many arguments, with the girls not agreeing with one another. Observing your children at war is quite painful as a mother. Many things were voiced that should not have been, as is often what happens in the heat of an argument. Emotions run high and lashing out to hurt someone that is hurting like you is usually the outcome, albeit the wrong choice.

At that time, I genuinely thought Emma and Amy were lost to me as they had such a strong bond with their father, whilst Jade supported me. I spent many nights crying on my own, wondering if I had made the right choice. The guilt was sometimes overwhelming as I blamed myself for my marriage break-up; after all, it was me who walked away. The consequence was that my relationship with my two older daughters became hugely complicated – how would I ever return from this awful situation? But I never badmouthed my ex-husband and that was one of the best decisions I have ever made. I had to think carefully before opening my mouth.

Watching Amy's pain and confusion was tough because she was such a daddy's girl and seeing her father upset caused her great anxiety. I wore kid gloves around her as she needed more careful handling. It was paramount that I kept her spirits high as much as possible, so she could find the inner strength to achieve her dream of becoming a teacher.

Jade

Jade, my baby, has followed in my footsteps by being a tomboy.

When Jade was in her second year of primary school, aged five or six, she was heavily into football with her best friend, Katherine. They were Leeds United supporters and wore Leeds United football tops. They were so passionate about the team that they had even been to a Leeds United football game at that age! We never gave it a second thought; it was just what Jade liked to do. Anything football-related and she was there, right in the middle of it.

On one occasion, parents had been invited into the school to watch an assembly. All the children were performing in some way; reciting a poem, dancing, or singing. Jade and Katherine decided to sing a Leeds United football song... so you can imagine the scenario! Their school was an extremely strict Church of England school, and in front of the whole school, these two very young, impressionable girls sang a rather inappropriate Leeds United football chant... Katherine's mother and father and Rob and I looked at each other, somewhat shocked, but also slightly amused that this had been their choice! I was mortified! The only saving grace was that, thankfully, the girls didn't know the exact words as some were rather rude and certainly not suitable for a primary school audience... We thanked God for small mercies, as otherwise, we might have found ourselves looking for another school!

At that time, we lived in Castleford but having been burgled a couple of times, we decided to move to the countryside. We wanted to give our girls a sense of freedom that the country offers over a town, with lots of fresh air and outdoor activities. We had a large paddock and when we asked Jade if she would like a pony or a motorbike, without hesitation she chose the motorbike... no surprise there! She loved active sports and also played golf. As a younger golfer, she was incredibly talented, playing for Yorkshire Girls with a handicap of 6 as a 14-year-old!

There were times when Jade's golf was our only priority, and the summer was taken up with the family walking around golf courses, supporting and encouraging her. My other daughters didn't have a say as we were a family giving our united support to our child who had a gift. Did Emma and Amy truly want to spend their weekends sitting in a car doing their homework or walking around a golf course in the rain? Probably not!

Jade struggled with her talent; when she didn't play well on one hole, it would impact the rest of her game. Her coach advised that we used the phrase 'SUMO' when this happened, being the acronym for **S**hut **U**p, **M**ove **O**n. However, SUMO is not advisable to a 14-year-old who has high expectations of the standard of golf. It annoyed Jade even more, and was like a red rag to a bull.

After a while, there was no more fun in playing, and then she got injured so stopped playing completely. My current view is that if you do a sport, you should do it because you enjoy it, but I didn't think like that about Jade. At the time, it was more about her talent and what she could do with it, rather than whether she enjoyed the game.

As you can see, my three daughters were all quite different. One was bossy and motherly, the other a princess, and the youngest super sporty. Of course, like all children, they soon shed those childhood activities and found their personalities and way in the world. But those childhood memories always make me smile.

Moreover, Jade was the one I was most dragged into school for because she didn't toe the line. She was quite a rebel at a young age. It was tough for Jade – she'd experienced many deaths in her younger days, including her uncle, grandad, and great uncles and aunts, all of whom were close to her; being a rebel was her way of coping. It's strange because I always thought it was to do with understanding her sexuality, but Jade tells me differently. I'm quite sad that I didn't realise her issues and she was too young to ask for help.

We knew Jade was different because she was very much into boys' things. We didn't push any gender toys or activities onto any of our girls; we believed it was their choice to play with what they wanted. When they got a little older, it was up to them how they dressed. Our job was to teach them how to treat others and to learn right from wrong. We only liked them to be girly girls when we went to a family wedding, where they would all cooperate and wear pretty dresses. Even Jade accepted this family tradition.

As Jade grew into a teenager, I was called into school over her disruptive behaviour. This in turn filtered into home life as Jade and Rob were at loggerheads, often butting up against one another.

I remember so clearly the day that she intimated she had a girlfriend. She had already left school and was now 17.

"That's fine. As long as you're happy," I said.

"Aren't you disappointed or anything?" she replied, a little bewildered.

"No, I always knew you were gay. It doesn't matter. It's entirely up to you what you do and who you go with. Whichever way you go, it's entirely your decision. All I want is for you to be happy."

She smiled and we carried on as usual.

The bottom line is that you want the children in your life to be healthy and happy. It is about accepting them, no matter what, and not having particular expectations. Weirdly though, I had never thought about my children's sexuality – it didn't cross my mind until Jade came along and I could see she was different. It certainly wasn't a big talking point in my childhood and teens.

The first time I came across different sexuality was on *Brookside*[4], a television soap on Channel 4. It featured a storyline about two girls in a lesbian relationship and showed them kissing, which was pretty risqué at the time. I remember that it caused a huge furore in the media too. Times have changed and people are now far more accepting of same-sex relationships, which in turn is reflected in television and film.

I had another conversation with Jade when my curiosity got the better of me, and I asked her why girls. She turned to me and said, "I am bisexual."

I asked her to explain that to me so I could understand, and it had nothing to do with judgement.

She explained, "Obviously, when I'm in a relationship with a girl, it's the person I love. It's not about that person's gender. So boy or girl, if I love them, then that's all that matters. It's the connection, not whether they are a boy or girl."

To date, this is one of the best descriptions of sexuality and feelings that I have ever heard.

When I finally left the family home, Jade followed me to live at my parents' again until I found my feet. She was still figuring out what to do with her life and choosing a career path and flitted from one thing to another. Once again, this had much to do with her struggle to find herself, her sexuality, not knowing herself, not knowing what she wanted to do. Struggling with her identity was challenging for both of us; I was sad to see her so unsettled. All you can do as a parent is offer reassurance that all will be well and to be available for them when they need you for anything; a shoulder to cry on, or any other emotional crutch they need.

It took quite a few years for Jade to settle. She didn't want to go to university but she was offered the same opportunities as her sisters. She could have gone to university if she had wished. By not going down the higher education path, Jade then had other opportunities that her sisters did not have. There's no right or wrong choice; it is more about the choice that works for you.

She tried various different jobs and found nothing that suited her skill set or personality. Then she found a friend, and a long-term relationship ensued followed by her marriage. However, sadly, like me, the marriage didn't last. Life doesn't always work out the way you think it will, as I knew only too well. It was going through this experience that helped her understand her own true identity and acceptance. She finally realised that she had nothing to prove to anybody. She began to settle and her career took off. Jade now works in sustainable energy, and she's progressing her way up the ladder.

Often, as a parent or someone who has a child in their life, you have certain expectations, but I have learned that expectations can cause pain if the child doesn't live up to your dreams for them. They have their **own** dreams. Mothers may give life to their children, but it is not their life to live. In fact, part of the gift of life is to let them live, to find their own path, to make their own mistakes and learn from them. A mother's love is always there for them when they stumble and reach out for loving support and guidance. Accepting your child for who they are is all you can do.

Finally, motherly love is something you feel on the inside and demonstrate outwardly in your words and actions. It is always potent, but how you respond to it in different relationships can be diverse. No doubt I suppressed it at 15 giving birth to my son, who was cruelly taken away from me and was then robbed of it with the miscarriage. However, I embraced it in its fullness when I gave birth to each of my three girls.

When I reflect on the relationship with my mother, did I, as the child, feel or understand motherly love from her? Perhaps not in the same way that I consciously chose to display affection to my children, but in her way, like each of us, she did.

The cycle of life is extraordinary. One moment you are a child receiving unconditional love and learning how to give it back in return, and the next, you are the mother experiencing it in all its glory.

One thing for sure is that when grandchildren come along, it is a gift that keeps on giving. It is endless and limitless; that is what I have learned about motherly love. And it continues long after you are gone.

Summary

You can't live your child's life for them. You need to let them make mistakes, as we all learn from our mistakes. Giving the foundations to help them grow and blossom, and become independent, is the greatest gift ever. I have a beautiful photograph album that the girls put together for me. There is a lovely photograph of all of us at Christmas time, sitting around a table eating Christmas dinner with the annotation, "Family is where love begins and family is where love ends."

Yvonne's Top Tips

- When bringing up children, you need to set the boundaries; but remember, like anything in this world, the boundaries can be moved – it is not a sign of weakness, but of strength.

- How many of you take photographs on your phones but never look at them, or delete them because you've not got enough memory space? Give a gift of a photobook: add photographs that mean something meaningful to you both and write a special message below the photograph. In years to come, it will be looked at with a smile and maybe a loving tear.

- Don't be afraid to show your feelings in front of the children in your life; if you are sad, then explain why. Being honest and showing your emotions will help your bond, build on your relationship, and reduce stress and anxiety overall.

Memory Box 4: Limitless Sleep – Death Is Not the End

Family

It was 21st May 2000 – a lazy Sunday filled with joy and celebration. We had just returned from a delightful christening ceremony for our close family friend's precious child, and the day had been a whirlwind of laughter and love, leaving us content and ready to retire for the night. Little did we know that this seemingly ordinary Sunday was about to take an unexpected turn that would change our lives forever.

As the children peacefully slept, I nestled cosily in bed, appreciating the moment's peace. Suddenly, a knock on the door resonated through the house, shattering the stillness of the evening. Rob went downstairs, leaving me snuggled up in bed.

As Rob opened the door, a sense of anticipation filled the air, and what awaited him on the other side was beyond anything we could have imagined. The atmosphere seemed to crackle with tension as I strained my ears to catch any hints of the unexpected revelation that was about to unfold.

To my astonishment, Rob returned with an expression that hinted at something meaningful. He stood there, gazing at me, and I could see that he was struggling to find the right words to repeat the newly delivered message. It was as though time had frozen, and the weight of the unknown hung in the air, enveloping us in its mystery.

Finally, Rob mustered the courage to speak, and what he revealed left me speechless. Our lives were about to take a dramatic turn, the knock on the door the catalyst for a series of events that would completely reshape our lives.

Having enjoyed our day, we had been oblivious to the news on TV. The devastating news that a tower crane had collapsed, claiming the lives of three men. The three were using a climbing frame incorporating a hydraulic lifting device, to raise the height of the tower crane. However, the crane and tower overturned and all three men fell more than 120 metres.

One of them was Martin, my beloved brother, who was only 31 years old, just 18 months younger than me. I was absolutely devastated and heartbroken. This tragedy that left us all grappling with grief and disbelief, knowing he had so much life ahead of him, a life now tragically cut short.

As a family, we felt an overwhelming need to witness the site where this terrible event had unfolded, so a few days later we travelled to Canary Wharf in London, not knowing quite what to expect. The moment we arrived, the gravity of the situation struck us like a tidal wave. Before us lay a massive crater and, around it, the twisted metal of the fallen crane resembled a haunting labyrinth of spaghetti, a chilling reminder of the destructive power of fate.

But the most challenging part was yet to come. We visited the place where my brother's life had so abruptly ended. The reality of the situation engulfed us as we stood there, trying to process the incomprehensible loss we had suffered. As we approached, our hearts were heavy with sorrow, knowing that what awaited us was something no one should ever have to witness.

As if the scene of my brother's death was not enough, we then went to the mortuary. Behind a glass screen, we saw him – lifeless and still, his face marked by the impact of the tragic accident. The sight intensified our heartbreak and was exceedingly difficult to bear. We longed to hold him one last time, to feel his warmth, but we were denied the opportunity to do so. His body was covered in what appeared to be a protective cage and a cloth, which shielded us from the true extent of his injuries. We could only imagine the anguish he must have felt, gripping the crane as it plummeted towards the ground. It was impossible to shake the thoughts of how he must have felt in those terrifying moments.

The pain of losing him pierced my heart, intensified by the knowledge that he had left behind a young son and a loving partner, their lives forever altered by this terrible, heart-wrenching loss.

As we left that place of sorrow, I knew the memories of that day would forever remain, etched into our souls. The image of my brother, forever young and full of potential, will linger in our minds for a long time, a constant reminder of the fragility of life and the harsh reality of fate's fickleness. In moments of silence, I can't help but think of his dreams and aspirations, now forever suspended in time, a poignant reminder to cherish each day and hold dear those we love before the unpredictable hand of destiny intervenes.

The days following Martin's passing enveloped us in a mixture of grief and bureaucracy. In cases of sudden accidental death, a post-mortem is required. As a result, there was a delay in releasing the body, so the funeral could not take place until we received the necessary paperwork. It was a gut-wrenching wait, knowing we couldn't say our final goodbyes until all the official procedures were completed.

When the day of the funeral finally arrived, it was a sight that left me both stunned and overwhelmed with emotions. A sea of faces surrounded the church, each a testament to Martin's impact on many lives. The sheer number of people who came to pay their respects and support us was a testament to the love and connection he had fostered with others. It was like something out of a film, but the reality was far more poignant, as we mourned someone so dear and close to our hearts.

Martin's passing affected each of us in profoundly different ways. I found myself withdrawing into myself, struggling to articulate the depths of my grief. Rob, who had lost his best friend, faced internal struggles while trying to be there for me. Our parents, who had lost their son, navigated their grief uniquely. Dad became pragmatic, seeking answers as to why this tragedy had occurred, while Mum felt lost, mourning the loss of her baby boy.

As we tried to cope with this internal loss, we sought solace in one another, each trying to find the strength to move forward. Martin's partner and son were grappling with their grief too, dealing with their emotions privately.

The circumstances of Martin's passing brought another layer of complexity to the grieving process. Since it was an accident at work, health and safety inspectors and the police became involved. Their investigations were vital in uncovering what had happened and ensuring that such a tragedy wouldn't befall another family.

We eagerly awaited their appointments, hungry for answers and reassurance that no one else would have to endure the pain we were going through. We clung to the hope that the knowledge gained from their investigations would lead to better safety measures and prevent similar accidents from occurring in the future.

Amid this overwhelming grief, we found strength in one another and the collective support of our community. The healing journey was filled with ups and downs, moments of despair followed by glimmers of hope.

Together, we navigated through the pain and tried to honour Martin's memory by learning from his passing and cherishing the time we had shared with him. The impact of his loss would forever shape our lives, but we vowed to keep his spirit alive in our hearts and strive to create a world where no other family would have to endure the same heartache we had experienced.

◊◊◊◊◊

At this stage, the memories of my father and his passion for precision engineering are deep in my heart. He was trying to deal with the tragedy on a practical basis and find out as much as he could about the crane itself. He was interested in understanding the inner workings of cranes, especially the art of climbing them.

I remember a peculiar incident when health and safety inspectors visited our home with a model crane, hoping to shed light on the tragedy that had taken three lives. With his meticulous knowledge, Dad halted their presentation, pointing out that the crane in question wasn't the same type that had claimed the life of his son and two others. They left hastily, apologising for their mistake.

In the wake of this terrible accident, it was clear that the UK lacked crane experts to assist with the investigation. Health and safety officials were left struggling, gathering information from various sources without much progress. Feeling a sense of responsibility, I decided to conduct my own research, and my quest led me to an expert in San Francisco who had studied a similar crane collapse. I contacted him and he graciously agreed to help the Health and Safety Executive (HSE)[1] with their inquiry. I passed on his details, hopeful that this collaboration would bring much-needed clarity; however, the HSE decided to decline his help.

As the days turned into agonising months then years, we waited anxiously for the inquest to uncover the truth. The lengthy delay weighed heavily on Dad's health, and in August of 2003, just two months before the scheduled inquest, tragedy struck our family once again.

A massive heart attack claimed Dad's life and my world shattered into pieces. I vividly remember rushing home from work to find the ambulance outside. Against advice, I entered the lounge, only to witness the lifeless form of my dad as paramedics worked frantically to revive him. The sight remains forever in my memory, haunting me in my darkest moments.

When the long-awaited inquest finally convened in London, we sat there, hoping for answers, for closure. Despite days of deliberation, an open verdict was recorded. This means that the coroner and jury confirm the death is suspicious, but are unable to reach any other verdicts available to them. This left us with a swirling mix of emotions: frustration, anger, despair.

I couldn't contain my feelings, and as we emerged from the courtroom, I made a passionate statement to a reporter for BBC London, expressing my anger at the lack of accountability and the unanswered questions. All we wanted was to understand why the crane had collapsed, and, in our pain, we sought someone to blame.

The journey had been fraught with pain and sorrow, and the weight of our loss remained heavy on our hearts. The memory of my dad's passion, his untimely demise, and the quest for truth became integral to my story, driving me to seek justice and prevent others from experiencing the same heartache. Though our questions may never find satisfactory answers, I hope Martin's legacy will inspire change, ensuring a safer world for those who follow.

I couldn't see beyond my pain in the depths of my grief. The loss of my baby brother had torn a hole in my heart and my anger consumed me. I felt nobody could truly understand the devastation I was going through, not even Rob. It was all about me and my pain, and I failed to see the impact my brother's death had on the people I loved, especially my husband.

A few years later, fate offered me an opportunity that would unknowingly become a path to healing. I was approached to take charge of the health and safety requirements for a business aiming to secure a crucial tender. It was a challenging task, but there was a glimmer of hope amidst my grief. I decided to pursue a qualification with NEBOSH (the National Examination Board in Occupational Safety and Health), a step that benefited the business and, unexpectedly, began to heal the wounds in my soul.

The NEBOSH course was more than just a professional development opportunity; it became a journey of self-discovery and resilience. Delving into the world of health and safety, I confronted my emotions and slowly learned to cope with the loss that had shaken my world. The knowledge and expertise I gained became a beacon of light and a glimpse of how to move forward.

But amidst this new-found strength and purpose, my marriage bore the weight of our shared grief. The loss had taken its toll on both of us, and we found ourselves drifting apart. The pain was too overwhelming, and we struggled to find solace in each other. The strain on my marriage was profound, and we found ourselves in a place of distance and disconnection.

Yet, I refused to let my brother's death define the course of my life entirely. With the support of my new-found career and my new unearthed resilience, I began to take steps towards healing and personal growth. It was a bittersweet journey, one filled with both triumphs and challenges.

Reflecting on those turbulent times, I realise that healing is not linear. It comes in waves, ebbing and flowing like the sea's tides. My journey has been one of ups and downs, discovering strength amidst vulnerability and finding a way to honour my brother's memory while finding a path forward.

Amid it all, I learned to forgive myself for the moments when anger and grief consumed me. My heart is gradually opening up to the love and support around me.

I'm not afraid of dying;
I'm afraid of what I'm missing out on.
I'm afraid of being alone.

Grandparents

I vividly recall the tear-streaked face of my mum, and at the time, I thought her tears were due to the upheaval caused by the council's modernisation efforts in our three-bedroom council house. Our entire street was undergoing this transformation, and amid the chaos, I heard music for the first time beyond what Dad usually played at home. *Dancing Queen*[2] by Abba seemed ever-present, with workmen singing along as their radios blared while they worked away.

Amidst all this, we eagerly anticipated moving to a newly built house my parents would own. The council had agreed to postpone modernising our home until the very last moment. The conditions of the places were dismal, with my bedroom playing host to an unwelcome intruder – a large, brown creature that I initially mistook for a mouse, but quickly realised it was a rat... This discovery later led to a shocking revelation. In the adjacent house, a kind, elderly blind gentleman lived alone. His property was infested with vermin and they were finding their way into our home.

While the modernisation took its toll on my mum, she was also mourning the passing of her grandad, which only added to her emotional weight. I don't have memories of my great-grandparents, but I was fortunate enough to have known and loved both sets of my grandparents.

The loss of my grandparents came years later, and it was tough when my Nanna Lucy (my father's mother) passed away. I remember visiting her in the hospital, not fully comprehending the gravity of her condition. We shared a tender moment, and she asked me to rub her back before we said our goodbyes with a kiss.

The next day, I learned of her passing, and the sorrow of losing someone so dear to me overwhelmed me. Watching my father's father mourn the loss of the woman he loved deeply was heart-rending. Their love was a rare and beautiful bond I have never witnessed elsewhere.

As time passed, I found solace in my wedding photographs, grateful to have both sets of grandparents present on my special day. But life eventually took its toll and my Grandad Fred's health declined. He spent his final moments in a hospice, with the devoted care of Macmillan nurses. I was by his side throughout his cancer treatment, and as his life ended, he talked about his father, a topic he had never previously mentioned. I regretted not asking earlier, but I cherished our final conversations.

The loss of my mum's dad, Grandad, wasn't a surprise, as the hospital had called us numerous times, only for us to find him charming the nurses with his lively spirit. He was a character and our visits were always full of laughter and rugby stories. We chuckled when we arrived, as Grandma would warn us about his mood. It was a familiar routine – she would go to the kitchen to prepare a drink and he would slyly turn off his hearing aid, pretending not to hear her. His playful antics never failed to make us smile.

When Grandad left us, Grandma lived on her own for quite some time. She was a petite lady and I couldn't help but notice that her feet couldn't touch the floor while sitting on a settee. As time passed, life became more challenging for her. She lost her sight and started forgetting people, including me. Visiting her and seeing her struggle to recognise those she once loved was truly upsetting. Inevitably, death came for her too, and I hope she found peace in her final days.

The memories of my family's journey through life and loss are entwined threads in my soul, each moment a testament to the strength and resilience of the human spirit. We find love, laughter and the courage to move forward during life's trials. The passing of those we hold dear is heartbreaking and a reminder of the beauty of the time we share. Their memory lives on in our hearts, and through our journeys, we honour their legacy and find solace in the love they left behind.

The Unexpected

Have you ever experienced that feeling when something inside you dies? Sometimes, change within us happens over many years that we do not realise or sense that a part of us is dying. I experienced this many years after the birth of my firstborn child who, as you know, was cruelly taken from me. Others made decisions on my behalf because they felt I was too young, too immature and couldn't make the decision that was what they thought was 'right' for me. The toll of this trauma finally caught up with me.

Reactive depression[3] is depression that is caused "in reaction to" an external event or circumstance. In other words, it is a state of depression that people experience in response to significant stress, such as a break-up, the death of a family member, divorce, or workplace harassment.

I would soon learn about the impact of reactive depression in my life.

Trying to move forward with my life, I took every step possible to ensure my son had a chance to find me if he ever wanted to. My name was on the adoption register, my details were ready to be discovered, and my heart was open to the possibility of reunion. But there were lingering concerns, and my husband and I knew we couldn't keep this secret forever. We wanted to prepare our three girls, so they wouldn't be shocked if their brother reached out someday.

With shaky voices, we gathered our girls and gently explained that they had an older brother who had been adopted. We kept it simple, telling them that it would bring me immense happiness if he ever wanted to find me. Their innocent minds absorbed the news, and the next day at school, their excitement got the better of them. They proudly told everyone about their brother, and soon, the school summoned me to the headteacher's office.

Waling in, my heart raced as I wondered how the school would react. They were unaware of my son, but after explaining the situation, they understood and made a record. The girls, eager to share their news, told everyone they knew, including their grandparents. I couldn't help but wonder how that revelation went down without my husband or me being present.

I thought I had moved on and left the past behind me. But deep down, something was amiss. I would find myself driving, and out of nowhere, tears would start streaming down my face. I felt lost in my emotions, not knowing why I was crying or what triggered these overwhelming feelings. It was as if a cloud of sadness hung over me, shrouding my happiness from those around me. When Rob was at work, I would cry alone, concealing my pain from my him, our children and everyone else. Not wanting to burden them with my struggles, I kept them all to myself, locking my emotions away in a Memory Box behind a carefully crafted facade of a smile.

One day, the weight of my feelings became too much to bear, and I opened up to a close friend about what I was going through. I poured my heart out, trying to make sense of the sadness that seemed to have engulfed me. My friend, sensing the depth of my pain, insisted that I seek help and talk to someone who could understand what I was going through. With their gentle encouragement, I mustered the courage to make an appointment with the doctor.

Sitting in the doctor's office, fear and hope were my companions in equal measure. I shared my struggles, recounting the moments when the tears overwhelmed me and the facade of a smile became my shield. It was a relief to vocalise the pain hidden deep within me finally.

The doctor took the time to review my medical history, searching for any clues that could shed light on the origin of my emotions. Then came a pivotal question that the doctor asked: had I ever sought counselling after giving birth to my adopted baby? Hesitating before responding, I realised that I had never addressed the emotions surrounding that painful chapter of my life. I had been watching an episode of the soap opera *Coronation Street*[4] where one of the characters, aged 13, announced her pregnancy. Out of the blue, this seemingly innocent light entertainment triggered my reactive depression.

The truth was, I hadn't sought any form of counselling at the time. After the adoption, life moved forward and I was left to cope with the aftermath alone. I buried my emotions, hoping they would fade away with time, but they remained dormant, like a volcano, lurking beneath the surface, waiting for a chance to erupt.

As I shared my truth with the doctor, I began to understand that I needed to confront the pain of my past to give myself permission to grieve and heal. It was an awakening, a realisation that I couldn't keep hiding behind my smile any longer. The doctor offered me support and guidance, showing me I didn't have to face this journey alone.

I decided to seek counselling, delve into the depths of my emotions, and finally confront the pain I had been running from for so long. It wasn't an easy path, but I felt a glimmer of hope with each step, knowing that healing was possible. Embarking on this journey of self-discovery and healing, I had my friend's unwavering support, and, slowly, I opened up to my family as well.

The road ahead was uncertain, but I would no longer let my emotions consume me in silence. I learned that it's okay to seek help, embrace vulnerability, and let others in because sometimes, in our moments of honesty and rawness, we find the strength to heal and reclaim our happiness.

The doctor's recommendation for counselling left me feeling a mix of emotions – uncertainty, fear, hope. On my way home, I mustered the courage to share the truth with Rob, hoping he would understand the turmoil I was going through. But his surprise and shock only confirmed what I had suspected; he didn't truly grasp the depth of my hidden pain. He believed the smile on my face meant everything was okay, but little did he know what lay behind it: a well of buried emotions.

In the following weeks, I found myself drawn into the storyline of the character in *Coronation Street* – how she faced pregnancy and emotions similar to those I had experienced many years ago. It was like a trigger, unlocking memories I had buried for 17 years – memories of my teenage pregnancy and the painful decision made 'for' me to put my child up for adoption.

Counselling became a pivotal part of my healing journey, but my experience with it was strange and disturbing. The first session felt one-sided as if I was revealing more about the counsellor than myself. Even though I needed help, I didn't return. I couldn't shake the feeling of discomfort and vulnerability.

However, amid my counselling confusion, another door of support opened. My doctor introduced me to a group called After Adoption[5], where people like me, searching for their children or birth parents, could come together. Driving to the first session, I felt a mixture of nerves and anticipation. What was I getting myself into? My previous counselling experience hadn't gone well; would this be the same? But as I approached the venue, an unexpected sight caught my eye – the vision of the Virgin Mary on a cross. Although I am not religious, it felt like a sign, a comforting presence reminding me that I wasn't alone on this journey.

Stepping into the group, a room of women greeted me, all birth mothers sharing their unique adoption experiences. It was a space of understanding, compassion and shared pain. Each different story somehow resonated with my own; in those moments, I felt a connection that transcended words.

Listening to the stories of these strong, resilient women, I realised I wasn't alone in my struggle. They, too, had carried the weight of a profound decision and the burden of loss. In that group, I found a sense of belonging, where we could all openly express our feelings without judgement or fear.

The road to healing was far from easy, and the pain of my past still lingered, but in those moments of shared vulnerability, I had taken a crucial step towards reclaiming my truth and finding peace within myself. The journey was far from over, but surrounded by the support of those who understood my pain, I felt a glimmer of hope that one day, I would find the closure and healing I so desperately sought.

In that small room, surrounded by women who had endured decades of heartache and resilience, I couldn't help but feel like a time traveller. They spoke of their experiences during the 1950s, 1960s and early 1970s, when teenage pregnancies were stigmatised and shameful. Some had been reunited with their children, only to be met with rejection and pain. Others had spent years searching for their lost children, some even finding them as far as Australia. The stories varied and the emotions were raw – from heart-warming reunions to shattered hopes.

Listening to their narratives made me realise that their struggles were not isolated incidents. The news, too, was full of mothers' stories who were now demanding apologies over forced adoptions[6], and I couldn't help but feel the weight of history bearing down on me. I wasn't a teenage pregnancy of the past; my son was born in 1983 and somehow, I had slipped through a time where protection and understanding were lacking. In today's world, things might have been different; I might have had a voice and professionals who would have sat down with me and understood my deepest desires, not just those around me.

Though I attended several sessions with the After Adoption group, I often felt like a fish out of water. I was so much younger than the other women and my son was only 17 years old, making me ineligible to search for him under the law. But in my heart, I held onto the hope that one day he might want to find me, so I registered my details on the adoption search registrar.

The pain of losing a child to adoption was an unspoken heartache that transcended time. I carried the weight of those shared stories in my heart, knowing that despite the years that separated us, it was essential to weave our pain and longing into a tapestry of motherly love. Each woman in that room had endured the unimaginable, yet they displayed an unyielding strength that inspired me.

Though I couldn't find my place in those support sessions, I knew my journey wasn't over. I clung to the belief that someday, our paths might cross again. Until then, I would wait, my heart open and hopeful, ready to embrace whatever the future might bring.

As time marched on, the world began to shift, acknowledging the pain of forced adoptions and the need for healing. I longed for a future where no mother would have to bear the weight of loss alone, where understanding and support would be readily available. The journey towards closure was daunting, but I knew that by being open about my experience and seeking connection, I was taking vital steps towards healing my wounded heart.

With each passing day, I held onto the hope of reuniting with my son, envisioning a future where we could share our stories, heal our wounds, and build a new chapter together. Until that day arrived, I would continue to hold him in my heart, whispering my love into the universe and sending a silent prayer that someday, our hearts would find their way back to each other.

In the depths of my pain, I could only find solace by convincing myself that he was gone forever and that I would never see him again. It was a coping mechanism to shield myself from the unbearable ache of loss. I locked away those emotions in Memory Boxes, burying them in a hidden corner of my mind. Maybe it wasn't the healthiest way to navigate reactive depression, but it was the only way to survive.

Years passed and life seemed to move on. But the pain remained, lurking beneath the surface, waiting for the right moment to come up for air. And it did, triggered by the actions of another party, an event I am legally bound not to discuss. Once again, the smile returned to my face, the mask I wore to keep my struggles hidden. Behind closed doors, I cried alone, suffocating in silence.

On a spa night with a close friend, my emotions became too heavy to bear. I couldn't keep it all bottled up any longer and broke down, ruining what should have been a joyful evening. My friend saw through my brave front and urged me to seek help to talk to my partner about what I was going through. I agreed, but on returning home, fear held me back and I did nothing.

Days later, a conversation with Emma turned to the turmoil in my life and the floodgates opened once more. Emma, just as my friend has done, encouraged me to seek help to open up to my partner. It took me days, but I mustered the courage to speak with my doctor, even though it had to be over the phone due to the Covid pandemic.

As I cried to my doctor, answering questions about my emotions, I knew that my current situation had robbed me of control, leading to this resurgence of reactive depression. My doctor prescribed medication to lift my mood, but I continued to wear my smile to the outside world, concealing my pain.

My partner, unaware of my past struggles with reactive depression, walked in on me while I was talking to the doctor. He saw my tears, shocked and concerned. Though he had sensed something was wrong, he had no idea about my earlier battles. I want to thank my friend Claire and my partner for their unwavering support during this difficult time.

With their help and the medication, I gradually took back control of my life. The tears subsided and I found the strength to continue moving forward. While the scars of my past still lingered, I knew that with the love and support of those around me, I could navigate through the darkness and find my way back to the light. It was a journey of healing, resilience and learning to embrace the vulnerability that makes us human. I held onto the hope that the pain would no longer dictate my life one day, and I could find peace and contentment once more.

Then, one day, as if the universe was finally granting my wish, an email popped up in my inbox that caught my eye. My hands trembled as I read the words, my heart overwhelmed with mixed emotions. It was the communication I had dreamed of for so many years – my son had found me and wanted to connect with me! Joy and fear intermingled as tears streamed down my cheeks.

Questions and doubts flooded my mind: what if he blamed me for the past? What if he didn't like me? What if he didn't want to see me after all? I couldn't help but think back to those ladies at the After Adoption group, the ones whose stories didn't end as they had hoped. Their experiences lingered in my thoughts, casting shadows of uncertainty.

But despite my fears, I knew that I had to respond. I couldn't let fear hold me back from the possibility of a reunion with my son. With a deep breath and my heart in my mouth, I crafted my reply, trying to express the love and longing that had been tucked away in my heart all those years.

Pressing 'Send', I felt a mix of hope and anxiety. The journey ahead was uncertain, but I knew that this was a chance I couldn't pass up. It was time to embrace the vulnerability and take that leap of faith, taking the first step towards healing and reconciliation, no matter what the future held.

The day finally arrived: I was going to meet my long-lost son. I waited with bated breath, my stomach twisting with nerves and excitement, sitting in the restaurant. Scanning the room, my heart was pounding. And then, as if fate had intervened, I saw him walking towards me. I knew it was him instantly – tall, with a build reminiscent of my father and brother at the same age. With his fair hair and striking blue eyes, he carried the very essence of our family genes. My heart swelled with overwhelming emotion, and tears of joy threatened to spill. What a moment – one I will **NEVER** forget until the day I die.

Here he was, not the baby being taken away from me, but a grown man, forging his path in life. We talked for hours, the floodgates of curiosity opening wide. I had many questions about his life and journey, and he wanted to know all about his sisters and my husband. There was no blame, no resentment, only a sense of connection that felt like coming home. His adoptive mother had kept her promise and told him about me, allowing us to embark on this beautiful reunion.

As we parted that day, we agreed to stay in touch and continue building our relationship. And true to our word, we met again and again, our bond strengthening with each passing day. I was privileged to meet his adoptive family – his caring, loving parents and brothers. They welcomed me into their lives with open arms, and I couldn't be more grateful. They had raised him with love and support, and I knew he was in good hands.

My son had grown into an incredible man – grounded, well-educated and athletic. He had an excellent partner by his side and, a few years later, he became a father himself. Seeing him embrace fatherhood filled my heart with joy, knowing he would give his child the love and care he had received through his adopted parents.

And as for my daughters – well, they adored him from the moment they met. He became their protective big brother, offering guidance and support whenever they needed it. Our family felt whole again, and I knew how fortunate we were. The adoption path led us all to a place of love and connection.

I often think about how things could have been different, how easily our lives could have taken a different turn. If it wasn't for my son's partner's persistence in questioning his family history and health, and his determination to learn more about his past, we might never have found each other.

Life had brought us back together, and I cherished every moment. My heart filled with gratitude for the love and support that surrounded us. I knew that, no matter what the future held, we would always be family, bound by a bond that transcended time and distance.

Although I had tried to pretend he was dead, I knew this death was not the end. My son was back in my life, and this was a rebirth of family connection and love.

Death of a Career

Bullying doesn't just happen in the playground. As an adult, I worked for someone who would shout at my managers, yet he never yelled at me. Every time there was a meeting, a manager would resign due to his yelling. I worked in social care, as I continue to this day, and this particular owner told me to cut the food budget and drop the staffing levels in a care home. I was especially concerned about this instruction. The care home was already running on a shoestring.

Anxiety raged within me – I needed the job and the wage! My future depended upon my job! I submitted a proposal one Friday with reduced staffing, still feeling confident the care home would still be safe.

To my dismay, he rejected my proposal and told me to come up with something different for him by Monday morning, and then initiate it. The reduction in staffing triggered an inspection by the regulators, who said if we could not raise the levels immediately, they would close the home.

I spoke to the owner immediately, and in an instant, he agreed to a turnaround and increased the staffing levels to where they were before. However, as soon as the regulators left, he told me in no uncertain terms that the regulators did not run the business and that I had to cut the staffing levels once more. In a quandary once more, I knew the dire consequences of cutting staff, yet I did the owner's bidding.

The regulators then put the home on suspension because of this action. Against my better judgement, I attended meetings alone. After the sessions, I cried in my car and had no support. This heartless man owned the business, and in his intimidating manner and no uncertain terms, I had to obey the instructions.

After one particular challenging meeting, which he did attend with me, he could only sit in silence. He showed up as the weak man he was and never said a word at the meeting; it was me who answered every question. Again, I got in my car and cried.

Life was on a downward spiral. My marriage had broken up so I was alone. Desperate but determined, I asked for a meeting with the owner to discuss what had happened during the session. He said, "Did you feel like a lamb to the slaughter?" I was confused. He said, "I have to look after my properties and the business, not those who live or work in them."

I simply could not believe my ears! I tendered my notice and left. I could no longer work for someone who was a bully, who didn't give a damn about people – either staff or residents – and where profit was their only interest.

I had learnt a life lesson in social care: there is no place in social care for bullies; in fact, there is no place in the workforce or school or any environment for bullies.

Leaving my job due to bullying made me reflect on which famous people had endured bullying. When I researched this question, I was very surprised. They include but are not limited to:

- ✓ Kate Middleton
- ✓ Eminem
- ✓ Lady Gaga
- ✓ Michael Phelps
- ✓ Justin Timberlake
- ✓ Victoria Beckham

When we look at this list, the one thing that stands out is that, in some way, they have all learnt to live with what happened to them, and they have not let it hold them back. They have all lost something, be it a job, self-esteem or confidence, like me. Sometimes, losing something we care about, such as our job, especially through bullying, can feel like a death. But life experience teaches us that we must carry on. The world does not stop for those whose time it is to leave it.

It is the same with your job or career. There is always something better, different and more challenging that can give back your self-esteem, belief and confidence. There was for me. I still work in social care, but have put into practice everything I have learned.

Death of a Marriage

In the beginning, none of us embark on the journey of marriage with the expectation that it will end. We all dream of being happy ever after, believing our love will conquer all. But life has a way of unfolding unexpectedly; sometimes, even the strongest bonds begin to fray.

As time passed, questions started swirling in my mind. Had I changed, or had we simply drifted apart? Trust is the foundation of any relationship, and it was becoming painfully clear that neither of us had that trust anymore. The distance between us seemed to widen, leaving us feeling lost and disconnected.

It was the little things that chipped away at our love. One particular annoyance was Rob's constant swapping of TV channels. It may seem trivial, but it felt like a symbol of our growing disconnect. He didn't seem to realise how inconsiderate it was, how it disregarded my feelings, or that I was engrossed in something enjoyable and interesting. That seemingly insignificant act tipped me over the edge.

The tension reached its breaking point and emotions erupted within me. I couldn't contain my frustration any longer, and a heated argument unfolded in a flash. Each word was exchanged like a dagger piercing the heart of our once blissful union. As the voices rose and emotions swirled, I knew I had to escape the turmoil.

I couldn't bear to stay in that suffocating atmosphere any longer, so I walked out, seeking solace and refuge in the familiar embrace of my mum's home. It was a bittersweet moment, leaving behind a life I had cherished and seeking comfort in a place that always felt like home.

That fateful night marked a turning point in my life, as I faced the stark reality of my unhappiness and the painful decision ahead. I had to leave behind what was once our family home and start over again. Seeking refuge in my old childhood room, I couldn't help but feel the weight of insecurity settle upon my shoulders. At 45 years old, I found myself in a familiar yet foreign place that was once home but now belonged to my mum. I felt hopeless, yet still had a roof over my head, feeling lost in a realm of contradictions.

In the quiet of my mum's house, I found a moment of respite to reflect on my marriage. The weight of uncertainty rested heavily on my heart as I questioned whether our love could withstand the storm we found ourselves in.

None of us could have predicted the twists and turns that led us to this point. As the days turned into weeks, I grappled with my feelings, searching for answers and trying to make sense of the turmoil within. It was a roller coaster of emotions, filled with heartache, doubt and the desire to salvage what remained of our once vibrant love.

In moments of solitude, I remembered the cherished memories we had created together. Our love story was a tapestry of laughter, shared dreams and moments of tenderness. But the threads that held us together began to unravel somewhere along the way.

The path forward was uncertain, and I knew it would require courage to confront the truth and make the necessary decisions for our happiness.

During my turmoil, I couldn't ignore the profound impact my choice had on my children. It was heartbreaking to witness their confusion and struggle as they navigated their loyalties. I loved each one of them with all my heart, but my decision to break up the family home left them uncertain. From the outside, we may have appeared like a typical, happy family, but behind closed doors, I was battling my demons – lost, unhappy, and caught in a storm of constant arguments.

While returning to the safety of what I knew might have been the easy choice, I couldn't ignore the truth that it would not lead me on the path to happiness. I spent countless hours alone in my old room, where tears flowed freely, questioning my future and what it held for me. It was a painful realisation to admit that I loved Rob, but not in a way that could guarantee a happy ever after. My love for him stemmed from his role as the best father to our children, and it was a bond I would always cherish.

Throughout the process, I resolved to maintain my dignity and not speak ill of him in front of our children. Knowing how difficult it was for them to witness their parents' relationship unravel, I wanted to shield them from unnecessary pain. I didn't want them caught in the crossfire of choosing between Mum and Dad, a burden no child should bear.

It wasn't easy; my daughters longed for the familiarity of having Mum and Dad together again, and their yearning only added to my internal struggle.

My relationship with my two eldest daughters was tense; every interaction felt like walking on eggshells. Yet I remained hopeful that we could rebuild our connection with time and understanding. Jade, my youngest, came to live with me and Mum, and her presence provided comfort and support during those trying times.

Amid this emotional storm, I tried to ensure that family events were not awkward or uncomfortable for those around us. I wanted to preserve a sense of normality and show the world that life goes on despite our challenges.

But deep down, my heart ached for a sense of peace and happiness that seemed so elusive.

Embarking on this new chapter of my life, I held onto the hope that by finding my happiness, I could ultimately be a source of strength and inspiration for my children. Though the road ahead was uncertain, I remained steadfast in my determination to navigate it with grace and resilience, guided by the love I held for my children and the unwavering belief that one day, we would find our way back to a place of peace and contentment.

The end of a marriage is similar to the pain of death. When my marriage ended, it was not just the loss of the marriage that ripped my heart apart, but also the loss of other family members and friends. Unintentionally, people take sides; some who had been family friends for all those years were now strangers.

Life's journey is unpredictable, and we must find the strength to navigate its twists and turns with grace and resilience.

Summary

Don't shy away when speaking to children about death. Seek help if you need to. Be honest and answer questions.

When my brother died, we needed to explain death to our girls who were extremely young at the time. We were fortunate to have a vicar who helped by narrating

The Story of the Dragonfly[7], the story of the water bugs that turned into beautiful dragonflies, who when they left the pond, could never go back.

Yvonne's Top Tips

- My children have all been told that whatever decisions you make in life, you have to live with them. The easiest decision of all is the one where you don't make a decision; you stay where you are, or you don't make any changes. Ask yourself the question: in the long run, will I be happy? If not, do something about it.

- Do you find yourself crying alone, putting a smile on your face to the outside world but feeling numb inside? Do you hide your emotions? If you do, please reach out for help, confide in a friend, or ring your doctor. There are also lots of helplines to speak with someone and find your support.

- Have you ever tried writing things down, and making a list of all the positive things that have happened to you? Spend time reflecting and reminiscing about those good things rather than simply the negative aspects.

Memory Box 5:
That Bloody Woman!

T hat bloody woman" is a phrase about significant women in my life who have taught me lessons and influenced me. Some of these lessons will be positive, from women who have had a significant impact on my choices for the better. Some are women I wished had not entered my life and who are now no longer not part of it, while others are women I welcomed with open arms. However, one learns from both negative and positive experiences. Always remember, it is up to you what you do with those experiences.

Social Worker

In 2001, I decided to leave my details on an adoption register so that should my son ever want to find me, he would know where to come. I also contacted the social services that had dealt with the adoption, to try and see my records to help me understand what had happened.

A lady from social services came to my house with the records. They couldn't be sent to me directly and any reference to my son's new name or birth family were removed. She handed me the records and let me read them there and then, as I wasn't allowed to keep them. She then told me that I already had a copy of an accompanying letter, as well as a photograph. My face must have been a picture of confusion as I had no idea what she was referring to!

She handed me a copy of the letter, which was addressed to me. It was from my son's adopted mum. The letter was the key to unlocking the door that had been closed for all those years, the years of wondering and not being able to answer questions. The letter was beautiful; it told me my son would retain his Christian name, that he would be loved, and that he would always know about me and the circumstances behind the adoption. However, there was no copy of the photograph.

Once she had left, I went straight to my parents' house. I was SO angry. Why had this letter and photograph not been shared with me? After all, it was addressed to me! Mum and Dad knew that I wanted to find my son, but they were grieving for the loss of my brother Martin.

I asked Mum for "my letter" and she understood straight away, responding with something that I have never forgotten but I truly understand now why; it was grief. Her response was, "That bloody woman should never have brought it... how do you think I feel, losing my son and you're looking for yours?"

Mum had the letter and a photograph of my son as a baby; he was so beautiful and I'd never even seen him. When I asked why they hadn't given me my letter and photograph, she said that the time had never felt right and that she was going to give it to me before I got married, but then she didn't want me to be upset on my wedding day!

I was absolutely devastated and told Mum that it wasn't her letter and photograph to keep and that she should have given it to me. On the other hand, I didn't want to even consider the possibility of falling out with my parents. I kept my distance from them for a while, needing to heal and not make a decision that I would later regret, that could have changed our relationship forever.

Betrayed Trust

I don't have that many friends because I've learnt to protect myself.

Rob and I were going through a rough patch and the girls and I were at my mother's house. My brother's death was affecting me deeply and life was taking its toll. Rob and I were constantly arguing; I was subsumed with grief and became insular and shut myself away from him. Neither of us knew what the future held and whether we would get back together. We decided to try again with Rob confessing to a dalliance; however, he wouldn't admit who the person was. And the problem with telling a half-truth is that it then becomes an issue of trust, eating away at you. From that point onwards, I didn't know who to trust. It wasn't until our actual separation that he confessed to it being my childhood friend...

Being betrayed in my marriage by a childhood friend is a bitter pill to swallow. Eventually, Rob came clean, but it was too late; our marriage was over. The whole episode had an impact on how I dealt with future romantic relationships.

Friendships

I can't remember a time when Cary wasn't in my life. I met her several years ago while playing golf. At first, I didn't understand her and thought her quite rude and a bit strange. People usually answered me when I spoke to them, but she seemed rather aloof, as if she was in her own world. Neither did she show her personality through smiles or facial expressions. She simply focused on her game of golf and nothing else, although at times she did tend to chatter about the most obscure things. It was rather challenging to get through to her. I decided that I didn't like her – but how wrong was I?!

During our game, I'd talk to Cary across the golf course but she didn't always acknowledge me. My mind would run wild as I wondered why she was not answering me. However, during one particular game, the penny dropped. She must have turned her head a certain way because it was then I noticed that she wore a hearing aid. I had got it completely wrong! The reason she didn't speak to me was because she didn't always hear me, as it depended on whether I was on her 'good' side when speaking to her, or which way the wind was blowing! The phrase "Don't judge a book by its cover" sprung to mind. It is so easy to make the completely wrong assumption and end up with egg on your face...

Cary is the most independent woman I know, living on her own and enjoying her own company. She gives so much of herself to the people she surrounds herself with. I see a true friend living life to the full, in the best way she knows how. A strong and driven woman, Cary has experienced life dealing with her partial deafness. I believe that her condition instilled in her not to judge others. It is not until you fully get to know someone that you can safely form a sound judgement on their character. Many people are too quick to assume, but the fact that she never judges me is what I love about her. She is, and always will be, one of my closest friends.

When my marriage ended, Cary was there for me. She was someone to talk to – I had learned to talk to her in the right ear and if I didn't, she politely reminded me to move around to the other side. Cary is an exceptional listener and no matter what I had done, she would not judge my decisions. What was wonderful about her was she often questioned me as to what had led me to a particular decision.

It is so important in life to not jump in too quickly, but to take time to reflect on situations and what decisions you may make. Often when you take time, you make better and wiser decisions that lead to a better outcome.

Despite Cary having a sensitive and serious nature, she has a mischievous and fun side. She will do anything for her friends, with no expectations of anything in return. If she inadvertently upsets someone, she questions herself and goes out of her way to put it right. On many occasions, we have led one another astray, normally when alcohol is involved... It was Cary who encouraged me to go out again to let my hair down after my marriage had ended. If she were here right now, I'm sure she would say it was me that led her astray! We are both as bad as each other!

A golfing weekend away turned out to be one of those occasions. The golf course was near Bradford, West Yorkshire, a beautiful location surrounded by hills and some of the old mill towns; the views were amazing. We decided we needed the exercise so we would walk with our golf trolleys. We should have realised it was a tough track as when you had to get to the first tee via a golf buggy, with someone taking you and your golf gear up the hill, it is a clear giveaway. The course was hard and undulating, and we were used to playing flat courses. It took its toll on our game with a couple of balls lost and scores that didn't reflect our true game. We were so glad to finish the course!

That evening, we blew caution to the wind and drank far too much Prosecco, talking with anyone and everyone, outstaying our welcome in the bar. The next morning, breakfast was a quiet affair, with Cary finding a quiet corner to read the newspaper.

I felt extremely rough; I had a hangover and I wasn't looking forward to trudging around the golf course again. I decided not to walk and used a golf buggy, riding around the course and only getting off it to hit my shots on the fairways and putt on the greens. Cary, on the other hand, decided there was no way she was using a buggy. She walked, although at times she would jump on the passenger seat holding onto her golf trolley as it was pulled along, not golf etiquette!

It was one of the many bad days at golf. I totalled up 13 balls lost and dread to think what my golf score was, but the views were good! We should have known better, but you are never too old to let your hair down and let your inner child escape!

Today, Cary is the little voice that makes me reflect on some of the bad decisions I've made. She never judges, but tries to understand. She lives life to the full. I've never known anyone with such a full diary but it does mean that booking in advance with Cary is always recommended. Cary is the type of friend who even if you haven't spoken in months, when you pick up the phone, it is as if you saw each other yesterday. I suppose that's the reason Cary has lots of friends, whether they are golfing, running, walking, cinema or holiday friends.

Friendships don't happen overnight and you do need to nurture them to ensure that they grow. If life has taught me anything, it is not about the quantity of friends but rather the quality. One or two great friends are all you need in life. "That bloody woman" Cary is a real gem and she has had a significant positive impact on my life.

Mum

The world would be a different place if we were all perfect, but we're not...

Mum made decisions that she believed to be right at the time, as I have done with my children. We want our children to learn from our mistakes, but we also want them to learn from their own mistakes.

I remember always wondering why my mum never learned to drive. Perhaps it was a sign of that generation when it seemed that more men than women drove the family car. I often asked her why she hadn't learnt. She thought that driving was the "man's job" and she didn't see the point of her learning! Although, today, I wish she had learnt because it would make her more independent and less reliant on those in the family who can drive.

My dad would go away for two weeks of the year, walking along the English coast with some of his friends. This was his opportunity to do what he loved, and be "one of the boys". One year when he was away, I remember begging my mother to cut my hair. Dad would never allow me to have my hair cut short but I was persuasive, badgering Mum like a broken record! Mum finally gave in and got the scissors out. My long blonde locks fell onto the kitchen floor – I now had a trendy short hairstyle!

When Dad returned home, he was furious at both of us. He was not a shouter, but being a college lecturer, he had a way of speaking that you could not ignore. He was a real disciplinarian! But he realised he could not 'undo' the act of cutting my hair. When I reflect now on my mum's brave decision to do something that went against his wishes, it showed her strength of character that was often hidden right up to the time of my dad's death.

Thinking about hair, and decision-making, I remember when Dad passed away, in a matter of a few weeks Mum went to the hairdresser and made the decision to cut her long hair. It turned out she didn't even like long hair, and it was only that length because that's how Dad liked it! She came home with a beautiful bob style that suited her. To this day, her hair has stayed short!

I won't ever forget seeing Mum running around after Dad, ironing his clothes and getting them out for him before he went to work or the pub. Every night before Dad went out, he would be dressed in jeans and a shirt, sitting in the chair ready to put his shoes on; he never got them himself! "Janet, fetch me my shoes," he would say, and, being the dutiful wife, she would always assist. Having seen her endure this for many years, I was adamant that I would not be 'fetching' shoes for any man!

Mum had true loyalty and devotion to Dad's old-fashioned ideas regarding a man and woman's role in the family. I guess both my parents were products of their generation.

I look at my mum now and see a lady who at times frustrates me, but at the end of the day, is my mum and nobody can or will ever replace her.

Female Relationships in My Career

In your working life, you meet many different people. Some will hold you back, while others encourage you, cheering you on. It was no different for me when I entered the social care industry. I came across women who challenged me in a negative way and others who were a positive influence on my decisions going forward. Like all jobs, sometimes you win and sometimes you lose. It is essential not to beat yourself up when things don't go according to plan. It is often because there is something bigger and better waiting for you around the corner. Let me share some of my stories working in social care.

Working in a residential care home as an administrator was the beginning of my career in social care, a career I love. I was an administrator working four hours a day, Monday to Friday. I was blessed with an operations manager who encouraged me to be the person I am today, putting her trust in me when the care home manager was off sick during a difficult time as the care home was to close, which meant those living in the home would move to an extra care housing scheme. Although new to the industry, with no training or qualifications, I was encouraged to pick up the reins of the manager (sadly never in title nor pay!). However, stepping up as I did, put me in good stead over the years and gave me an excellent grounding in the world of care.

I was encouraged by the operations manager to apply for a job, which would have meant a promotion and more money which, as a family, we needed. I was excited about applying for the job and gave the interview my all, but unfortunately, did not get the job, much to the amazement of my operations manager.

She encouraged me once more when another position arose. I attended the interview and it was the same lady interviewer as before. I thought it had gone well but once again, I did not get the job. My operations manager could not understand the reasoning behind it as by this time, I was experienced and knowledgeable enough. I put it down to not being 'the right fit'.

Just because I might not have been good at the interview, didn't mean that I couldn't have done the job – in fact, it is easy to recruit someone on the back of an excellent interview and then find out some weeks/months later that they are not as experienced or as good as you were led to believe! I didn't stay there much longer; it was time to move on as I needed more.

I look at my career now and think those setbacks were a blessing in disguise as I went on to do so many other things.

I was given an opportunity to be a trainer for a new social care provider, providing care to people living in their own homes; in the industry, this is known as domiciliary care. The group interview was at a nearby hotel. I nearly walked out though! Listening to others, talking about all their years of experience and knowledge, put doubt in my mind – I didn't believe I was good enough. The interviewer, Andrea, encouraged me to stay and put myself forward for the individual interview. To my surprise, I got the job!

Andrea encouraged me to push myself and was extremely supportive. My knowledge and confidence grew and I was promoted from Trainer to the Quality & Development Manager.

I was put forward for an award at the Great British Care Awards[1]. I was surprised to find out that I had been short-listed and would be attending the awards evening. I had never experienced anything like it before! I turned up wearing an evening dress with the men in black ties. The atmosphere was electric!

The awards began, the one I was nominated for being one of the last ones. My husband warned me not to get drunk as "you don't want to be winning an award and stumbling up to the stage!" so I stayed sober whilst everyone around me downed the wine on the table.

All of a sudden, my name was called out – I had won!! Having your name called out at the Great British Care Awards saying you have won is an exhilarating feeling!

I came off stage with my award in my hand and saw Andrea running down the aisle in her long evening dress to hug and congratulate me! She was clearly so proud of me.

A couple of years later, I was made redundant from a job that I loved. I am so thankful to Andrea as without her, my career would have gone in a different direction. She put her trust in me, for which I will always be extremely grateful.

Me

So who am I? The answer is, I am **ME!** It has taken me several years to fully embrace all of me but the journey has been worth it. If I can help just one person realise that it is okay to be yourself, learn to love yourself and stop being a people-pleaser, then this story is worth telling.

Like many of you, over the years I've not always liked myself, whether it is due to my yo-yo weight issues, my self-confidence, or the decisions I had made in my life. It is easy to carry the baggage of things in the past that weigh you down. If only you realised that it is okay to let it go. Life conditions you to conform and fit in, but the reality is that we are all unique and are made to stand out.

Sometimes you give the appearance of being confident, when inside you have not yet accepted who you are and have learned to wear a mask. As mentioned, I wore one for many years. Society expects that of you and it is easier to conform rather than please yourself.

At work, colleagues would see me as a confident individual. I am glad to say that this is now genuinely true, but there have been many times throughout my life and career when it has been all for show.

I am proud of what I've achieved and I believe I still have a lot more to offer. I do wonder where the 'Cas girl' (girl from Castleford) who dropped out of school with a couple of O levels, found this inner strength and determination to succeed in the world of social care.

Someone once said to me, "You're a Cas lass who came good."

I've not always been confident; in my younger years, I shied away from attention. Quiet and awkward amongst company, I never wanted to be the centre of attention. At parties, Rob, who was the life and soul of the party, used to deliberately leave me in a group of people hoping that I would engage in some kind of conversation. However, I chose to remain in the background and stay quiet, much to his frustration!

It was not until I took up golf in 2005 that I began to find a new feeling inside of me. It took winning a medal competition to finally unleash the 'competitive Yvonne'. I loved the feeling of winning and took confidence from those wins because I knew I had done something to the best of my ability. That is all anyone can ask of themselves in life. While winning is not always possible, it is a goal, and being part of a team is just as satisfying as winning.

Once you tap into your inner confidence, its ripple effect touches many other areas of your life. Having played golf for several years now, I am confident when playing with my friends. I have times when I beat myself up because my game is not good or does not meet my expectations. I know that it is not perfect every time and does not always go to plan, but it used to occasionally knock my confidence in a negative way. I have now learnt to take control; taking lessons put me back on track. This then spurs me on to be better the next time and I use that confidence to drive me forward.

I often wonder if this new-found competitive edge has leaked into other parts of my life, as my colleagues tell me I am competitive in my work. Pondering on this, I believe that it is because I strive for the best results, just as in my game of golf. I embrace this new trait because I am finally living my life in a way that fulfils me. Hard work brings results!

However, there are times when I have had imposter syndrome[2]. Imposter syndrome is a persistent, totally unjustified feeling that your accomplishments are undeserved. You doubt your abilities, despite evidence of achievement or respect, and are fearful of being exposed as being a fraud. This has made me miss opportunities, talking myself out of applying for a job or not putting myself forward to undertake a project.

The feelings of imposter syndrome come and go. I pressure myself to work harder to stop others from seeing my shortcomings, questioning my worthiness for the roles I have taken and worrying about being a failure. Looking at others, I question my intelligence, thinking that being a school dropout means that I am not as intelligent as my colleagues. I overcome this by working harder, for longer hours, setting myself goals, targets and ever-higher expectations.

However, I enjoy life to the full, as every minute matters. I once had a job for three months that I knew was not right for me after two weeks! But I stuck it out for three months to try and make it work. Towards the end, I couldn't stay there any longer and found myself counting the days to the weekend, counting down the days to my holidays; I was counting away my life, wishing it away. On returning from my holiday, we parted company much to my relief; I felt the weight lift off my shoulders.

Being a mum is the hardest job in the world! The hours are long, there is no pay, and there's an expectation that you know what you're doing! Well... I made it all up as I went along; I was a fraud! In those days, there were no apps and I certainly didn't have time to read any self-help books.

Decision-making as a parent is hard and you don't always get it right. How can you? Because sometimes you don't make the right decisions for yourself. What I do know is that you do put your children at the heart of those decisions and they are made with the experiences and knowledge you have at any one particular time. It is by making mistakes that you grow and make better decisions next time.

Summary

We should all remember that love isn't an automatic right. At times, my relationship with my mum has been difficult. We all have a "that bloody woman" somewhere; life can be full of negatives but if you choose to flip the lens, you can often turn them into positives.

My relationship with my girls when my marriage ended was also difficult but that said, I believe you get out what you put in. Think about what you say; remember others have feelings too, and most of all, remember that whatever you do in life, you have to live with the consequences. I've lived with lots of consequences as you will have realised by now, but I've come to terms with them. This has helped me to love myself, to understand who I am and why I have become the person I am, a content person who lives life to the full.

Yvonne's Top Tips

- Ask yourself the following question: are you being true to yourself? If you're not, then do something about it and make the changes.

- Who is your "bloody woman"? Like me, you may have several! Does "that bloody woman" have a positive impact on your life? If she doesn't, you need to move on.

- Speak to your closest friend and tell them how much they mean to you.

Memory Box 6:
A Can of Worms

Going Into Battle

My weight is a war against myself – a constant battle. These pages are imprinted with the experiences that shaped my body and my soul, as I journeyed from a carefree teenager to a dedicated mother of four children.

In the days when my teenage years felt like an eternity of endless possibilities, I wore my healthy weight with the innocence of youth. But as life unfolded, the landscape of my body transformed with the arrival of my first child. With a new-found independence, the allure of alcohol and the tantalising embrace of fast food soon became my companions. The edges of my waistline began to stretch, an unintended consequence of the freedom I had longed for.

Oh, the enchantment of independence, a siren's call that led me to embrace my growing curves! The familiar size 10/12 garments were replaced by size 14, yet within those numbers, I found happiness. Life brimmed with adventure, an unwavering love, and the symphony of freedom that echoed in my heart.

As the seasons of life shifted, my body embarked on the journey of motherhood once more. The arrival of my second child brought with it the challenge of morning sickness, a relentless companion that dictated what I ate. Jelly Babies and Caramac bars became my solace, providing a sweetness that countered the bitterness of nausea. With each passing day, my appetite grew as my body nurtured new life.

Baby number three was a different tune altogether. Morning sickness became a constant battle, playing out unpredictably at any given moment. Armed with bags that were ill-prepared for their task, I navigated the art of vomiting discreetly. My culinary preferences danced on a tightrope of contradictions, from bouts of sickness to cravings for Chinese cuisine. Hospital walls witnessed my struggle as my weight plummeted, a stark reminder of the fragile balance between health and chaos.

And then baby number four emerged onto the stage. Weeks of morning sickness paved the way for a crescendo of cravings, a chorus of appetite that harmonised with my expanding figure. With each passing day, my reflection in the mirror mirrored the joy of anticipation, as well as the physical transformation that accompanied it. Postpartum, I found myself at the crossroads of self-acceptance and the desire to regain balance.

As the years turned, I held onto gratitude for the resilience of my body. My journey was a testament to the spectrum of motherhood, marked by extremes of weight gain and loss. Amid these changes, I was fortunate that my children thrived and were healthy.

Through the lens of retrospection, I see the layers of my story intertwining – a narrative of growth, challenges and unyielding love. My body bore witness to the Memory Boxes of my life, adapting to the seasons of motherhood. This book is an ode to the journey, a tribute to the body that housed life, and a reminder that within the folds of change, the heart's embrace remains constant.

The British Nutrition Foundation[1] suggest that if you are already a larger lady, you need to be careful not to gain too much additional weight during pregnancy, especially if you have a BMI of 30 or over. Body mass index (BMI) is a measure that uses your height and weight to work out if your weight is healthy. Try eating healthily and keeping active if you can – a little effort each day goes a long way. As a result, you will have a more enjoyable pregnancy, reduce the risk of complications during pregnancy and childbirth, and have a healthier baby.

However, please, please remember that pregnancy is not the time to go on a diet! Normal weight gain is a result of your body changing to support the growing baby. Dieting could mean you are not getting all the nutrients that you need, meaning your 'bump' won't be getting them either. Crash diets or severely restricted diets may even harm your baby's development. It is important to focus on healthy eating and moderate exercise such as walking, rather than reducing your weight.

The amount of weight a woman may gain in pregnancy can vary considerably from person to person, but also from pregnancy to pregnancy. Only some of this weight gain is due to increased body fat, which is important to protect your baby and prepare for breastfeeding. There is also the weight of the baby itself, the placenta, the amniotic fluid and the extra fluid in your blood. Most of this weight gain happens in the second and third trimesters when your baby is growing and developing fully.

The most important thing is that being overweight can increase your risk of complications, such as gestational diabetes and high blood pressure, during pregnancy and childbirth. In addition, if you put on excess weight, it is much harder to get rid of after you have the baby.

I was and continue to be a typical yo-yo dieter; in fact, I can't remember ever being at my ideal weight. The highs and lows with the lows impact how I feel about myself. The overweight Yvonne is not a happy person. I lose my confidence, hiding behind baggy clothes and avoiding the camera. I put a smile on my face, although I still often cry. The crying is a release, a cry for help, but this cry is never in front of anyone else. I carry my weight well, putting weight on in proportion all across my body. Whenever I lose weight, although still not having reached my ideal weight, friends say, "Don't lose much more, you look well! Losing more weight will make you look drawn in your face." Although complimentary and meant kindly, these comments don't help as I've not met my ideal weight or my BMI!

I know my weight increases are due to my mindset at the time. My triggers are:

1. Boredom

2. Emotional stress and anxiety

3. Being unable to control the feeling of hunger

I have a secret eater in me, who can easily put away a packet of Custard Creams or a packet of five cookies from the local shop. My stomach has probably been stretched due to the large comforting food portions that I like to eat and as such, I don't feel full. And yet, I feel guilty, which then leads to a downward spiral.

I'd like to pretend that I love exercise, but it's quite the opposite, with the exception of golf! Golf is the only exercise that is a constant in my life. Some people believe that golf spoils a good walk (!) but I disagree – there's a lot to be said about both. Being outside, walking, swinging a golf club, chatting and laughing with friends for around four to five hours is good for the mind, body and soul. And it is usually far more than 10,000 steps!!

I've joined a few gyms over time; paid my money, had the induction, attended once or twice, then dropped out. The only losses I've had are from my bank account when the payments continued to go out. With all the goodwill in the world, I always intended to go back but never did. I bought myself a bike during lockdown in 2020, which I used for the first month or so. It now sits in the garage and only comes out when we visit Center Parcs or on the odd occasion when I have a pang of guilt!

At one particular low point, looking in the mirror, I didn't like what I saw so I decided to throw caution to the wind and look at alternative solutions to weight loss. After much research, I knew that I didn't want to go under the knife so I opted to have a gastric balloon fitted for 12 months. My weight and BMI meant that I was suitable for this procedure.

The procedure was quite painless and I was in and out in one day. I had hoped to watch the procedure on the TV monitor at the side of the bed in theatre; however, the sedative they gave me relaxed me so much that I fell asleep and only woke up when the surgeon had finished! It was neither painful nor uncomfortable.

Eating small portions worked – my weight dropped off, quickly at first and then it slowed down. I lost 2 ½ stone. The balloon inside my stomach was a sensation that I became used to, but I knew it was there at all times. Taking it out was as easy as putting it in. I continued to lose a small amount of weight and managed to stay stable for 12 months until we had an all-inclusive holiday. I put a substantial amount of weight back on that holiday and since then I have struggled. I certainly do not regret the operation, because even though it was costly, I was happy with how I looked. However, I regret not maintaining the weight loss.

One of my daughters said I was cheating! This was most certainly not the case! Why make it hard for oneself when there are alternatives out there for anyone struggling? I do have an excuse, in fact, several excuses for not exercising… I'm far too busy with work and anyway, big boobs and running do not go together! And in the winter months, when the fire is lit, it's cosy and warm so why would I want to go out!?

Let's face it; the only way to lose weight is to ensure you consume fewer calories than those you burn off; it's simple maths. I now have my new excuse as I failed maths not just once, but several times!

There will always be a fat person inside me waiting to be let loose. I have to be strong and in the right mindset to stop that person from taking over. There is one thing I do know: that person does not make me happy.

Menopause

Having had four children and being overweight had a huge impact on my health. At the age of 38, I knew I didn't want to have more children. This decision was accompanied by a feeling of guilt as my husband would have loved a son. However, with three girls, there was no guarantee the next child would be a boy. I was on the pill, the little tablet I'd been taking since my teens.

The contraceptive pill[2] has been called the greatest scientific invention of the 20th century. Invented in the sixties at a time of great change and social and political upheaval, it heralded a sense of freedom and choice for most women – to choose when to have a baby, to choose to have a career first, to choose not to have a baby at all. These were all choices that would have been almost impossible without the pill.

Deciding not to have any more children was difficult, but I was having major health problems; the types of problems that ladies in those days did not talk about.

My stomach hurt inside and to the touch, and I suffered from irritable bowel syndrome (IBS). It caused me to have stomach cramps, bloating and the embarrassing immediate need to go to the bathroom as I often had diarrhoea.

The IBS would come and go, sometimes lasting for days; one particular episode was so bad that it lasted a couple of weeks. The need to have a loo close by had an impact on my day and as you can imagine, the worry of not knowing when or where I would need the toilet caused me crippling anxiety. Although there's currently no cure, today my diet is much more healthy and I do not have any symptoms.

I was also diagnosed with a prolapse of my vagina wall and had stress incontinence; I was unable to exercise, cough or sneeze without wetting myself. I dreaded getting a cold or cough in the winter months. My legs would be constantly crossed whilst I coughed, trying not to wet myself. I was, in my opinion, too young to be wearing incontinence pads as they were for "old ladies". Instead, I would fold up toilet roll and put it in my pants as a precaution.

In my head, I would have conversations about the embarrassment of telling someone. Perhaps my cancerous cells had come back? Did I have cancer? Without seeing a doctor, I wouldn't know and the conversations in my head got worse and worse. However, I eventually screwed up my courage and booked an appointment with my doctor. Of course, the conversation wasn't as difficult as expected and with hindsight, I wish that I had taken the plunge earlier. My doctor was a female and extremely understanding and referred me to the gynaecological clinic. It was clear that my muscles were extremely weak; after years of neglect, they were unable to hold everything in place.

Certain things can increase the chances of stress and urinary incontinence, including pregnancy and vaginal birth, obesity, a family history of urinary incontinence, and getting older – although incontinence is not an inevitable part of ageing.

I ticked three out of the four…

Urinary incontinence[3] is the unintentional passing of urine. It's a common problem thought to affect millions of people. The NHS website states that there are several types including:

- stress incontinence – when urine leaks out at times when your bladder is under pressure; for example, when you cough or laugh

- urge incontinence – when urine leaks as you feel a sudden, intense urge to pee, or soon afterwards

- overflow incontinence – when you're unable to fully empty your bladder, which causes frequent leaking

- total incontinence – when your bladder cannot store any urine at all, which causes you to pass urine constantly or have frequent leaking

It's possible to have a mixture of both stress and urge urinary incontinence.

I was given a device to insert in my vagina to try to stimulate the muscles – and before you start smirking, it was a medical device, not a vibrator! (The vibrator became my friend years later when I was alone after my divorce – don't knock it until you've tried it!) The medical device worked but not enough to undo the damage. Pelvic floor exercises didn't make much difference either. The gynaecologist agreed that I needed a prolapse repair, a sling (vaginal mesh[4]) under my bladder and a hysterectomy, all at the same time. A strip of synthetic mesh was inserted behind my urethra to support it and would be permanent.

It was a scary thought, not helped by the disclaimer I had to sign, removing hospital responsibility if anything untoward happened to me while in the operating theatre. All three procedures were undertaken in one operation, meaning a three-night stay in hospital. I was not looking forward to it; this was no three-night holiday! I'd been in hospital for several stays before, including when I had my children and a traumatising tonsillectomy at 18 years old, where I cried whilst being wheeled through the corridors from the operating theatre back to my bed – I'd had an adverse reaction to the anaesthetic…

All three procedures took place, thankfully without issues or complications. I was given medication to ease the pain which ensured I was able to rest fully. I was extremely fortunate in that the mesh sling that was inserted never caused me pain or discomfort, unlike many other women who endured years of soreness and irritation. Recuperation from the operation was time at home taking it easy, not being allowed to vacuum, iron or do anything strenuous. The recuperation period can take up to three months for everything to heal, but the operation was a great success. I could now jump up and down, cough and sneeze, and no longer wet myself. I was cured! Hurrah!

After the operation, the ache in my stomach that came along every month had now gone forever. However, what I had not realised was that I would now go through the menopause … at 39 years old… There had been no discussions at any stage about the menopause and what impact this would have on my health, my mood and my later life.

I truly thought I had escaped the menopause symptoms that my mum endured; the hot sweats and the mood swings. Unfortunately, these typical menopause symptoms did affect me, including migraines that came out of nowhere. It soon became clear that I didn't have a full understanding of what the menopause was.

Menopause[5] usually occurs between the ages of 45 and 55 and is when your periods stop due to lower hormone levels. It can sometimes happen earlier naturally, or due to surgery such as a hysterectomy, cancer treatments such as chemotherapy, or a genetic reason. Perimenopause is when you have symptoms before your periods have stopped. You reach menopause when you have not had a period for 12 months.

Both can cause anxiety, mood swings, brain fog, hot flushes, night sweats and irregular periods. These symptoms can last for years and can impact your personal and professional life.

I am still living with some of the symptoms almost 20 years later. I take medication for migraines and cluster headaches, and as to the night sweats... I originally thought I was just hot and would throw the bedclothes off! I'd like to think I wasn't moody but my ex-husband would probably say otherwise, and this may well have contributed to my marriage breaking down. I had always thought of my weight being a factor in my sweating but I now realise it was a combination of both my weight AND the menopause. I would try and wear clothes that disguised my sweaty armpits.

Some 16 years later, aged 55, I started to experience other symptoms that, once again, ladies do not like to discuss. After several months of thinking these new symptoms would simply go away, I again plucked up the courage to discuss them with a health professional.

I dreaded having the most personal parts of my body examined, as I am sure every woman does. I had a vaginal discharge and occasional bleeding. A process of elimination took place, with vaginal swabs to ensure there was no infection and a vaginal ultrasound to ensure there were no evident problems, but all were clear.

I was diagnosed with post-menopausal symptoms[6] which had caused a thinning of my vaginal wall. The solution was HRT tablets and an oestrogen cream to be inserted into my vagina via a reusable applicator. It was a messy process and a hassle, as I had to wash it carefully after every use. I am sure that a woman scientist would have come up with a better solution than a reusable applicator! It was never completely clear of the cream when washed and was not really suitable. Eventually they prescribed an insertable tablet instead which was easier and more comfortable.

Summary

Day-to-day life sometimes means that we put our own health on the back burner. I remember Grandad put his own health issues to one side to care for Nanna when she was ill. Then after she had passed, he learnt that he had prostate cancer. We talk ourselves out of getting in touch with the GP, thinking that our symptoms will disappear.

As to women's issues, we know our bodies better than anyone else, which means there are times when you have to push to get the treatment you need from health professionals. The symptoms of ageing are not pleasant for any woman – so remember there is support out there.

Yvonne's Top Tips

- Don't wait too long with any symptoms. Seek help and make an appointment to discuss your symptoms with your GP. Do not be embarrassed – your doctor has seen it all before!

- Find a form of exercise that works for you – start small and remember that anything is better than nothing. See if you can get together with friends for an exercise class or play a team sport. Being with other people or part of a team can be much more fun, as well as having someone else to encourage you.

- If your weight is escalating, open up to those around you and ask for help. Take control of your eating. Start by writing a menu for the week and stick to it. When you go food shopping, make a list of the ingredients you need for dishes on your menu and don't be distracted by special offers and two-for-one offers!

- NEVER go shopping on an empty stomach!

Memory Box 7:
Finding Me

In childhood, I was nudged into the world of exploration by my parents, who ignited in me an enduring passion for the outdoors, nature and the countryside. The anticipation in the air was palpable at the crack of dawn on the first Sunday of each month. Mum meticulously packed our rucksacks, hiding treasures such as cold sausages wrapped in foil – my personal favourite – prepped the night before for our escapades across the breathtaking Dales. And I can never forget the magic of a flask of piping hot tea to accompany the delights tucked away in my backpack! To this day, my love affair with cold sausages endures…

Our family found a second home in the Yorkshire Subterranean Society, fondly known as the YSS. Dad's enthusiasm for walking led him to immerse himself in the club's activities. Dad's commitment became integral to our family life, from organising and leading walks to eventually assuming the role of President. Committee meetings, held in a room at the local pub, unfolded against the backdrop of spirited discussions fuelled, I presume, by copious amounts of Darley's ale. Little did I realise that this involvement would redefine our holidays, ushering in less time spent with Nanna and Grandad. This led to a bittersweet taste in my mouth.

As a 14-year-old, I experienced a holiday without Mum and Dad, revelling in the company of Nanna, Grandad and my youthful Aunty Trish. I had no idea that this would be the last of my carefree childhood holidays, as something unexpected had already begun beneath the surface – as you now know, I was unknowingly carrying a new life within me.

The initial forays into walking and camping with the YSS were exhilarating. We explored new horizons, revelled in the crisp air, and often found ourselves returning long after bedtime on Sunday evenings. Yet, over time, what once felt like an adventure became a routine, a Sunday morning obligation we no longer wanted to be a part of. Martin and I, yearning for lazy Sunday mornings, preferred the warmth of our beds rather than joining those early risers on the coach to the Dales. Childhood bliss and the appreciation of nature eluded us as we longed for lie-ins, the simplicity of children's TV and outdoor play with friends.

We were too young to see the beauty of the countryside and enjoy the wildlife surrounding us. Ironically, nature is something I now look forward to, and it fills me with awe and wonder.

However, as the adage goes, all good things must end. Our idyllic holidays with Nanna and Grandad ended and were replaced by adventures with friends who shared our YSS affiliation. We traversed the picturesque landscapes of the Yorkshire Dales, the Lake District and the Peak District, transforming from Sunday strolls to epic long-distance expeditions. The initiation to long-distance walking unfolded during the May spring bank holiday when, at the tender age of 12, I tackled the 81-mile stretch from Ilkley to Windermere on the Dales Way! In the rhythmic pace of our family holiday, Mum and Dad, the architects of our journeys, would meticulously fill our rucksacks with the essentials – scant clothing, dehydrated food awaiting water revival, a tent and sleeping bags. These weren't vacations in the lap of luxury; these were expeditions, a week-long odyssey without any comforts! As we set out, buoyed by enthusiasm, the sun bore down on us relentlessly, and the nearby river beckoned, its cool embrace tantalisingly close.

The Dales, a sanctuary of untouched beauty, unfolded before us. The river hosted a menagerie of life in its nooks and crannies along the bank. I witnessed my first kingfisher, a fleeting streak of electric blue dancing along the water before finding sanctuary on the opposite bank. The fields were alive with meadow flowers, a riot of colours, while lambs pranced, their exuberance echoing through the air. In their innocent play, they were oblivious to the harsh reality that awaited them, as Sunday lunch for someone…

Evenings offered respite for the adults in quaint pubs near our overnight stops, indulging in a ploughman's lunch or chicken in a basket. I, however, sought culinary adventure and insisted on trout in one pub, much to the scepticism of my parents. The grimace, the shiver and the tongue-sticking-out ritual that followed told the tale of my culinary misadventure! That night, a kind soul swapped meals with me, sparing me from a trout-induced famine. However, the distaste didn't linger, and today I adore all forms of fish and seafood.

A night in the cobbled village of Dent brought a change of pace. While our parents enjoyed the local pub, Martin and I, two mischievous scamps, opted for a knock-a-door run through the village streets. Our stealthy antics escaped retribution that night, leaving us with the thrill of adventure and a tale untold.

Yet, with each sunrise, the challenges of the journey loomed. Dew-kissed grass, noisy cows awaiting their morning milking – the country scene clashed with my teenage desire for extra sleep. When I questioned the early starts, the parental wisdom offered was, "The sooner we get started, the sooner we will finish." What that meant was, "The sooner we get started, the sooner we get to the pub!" Kids possess a keen perception that often eludes the grown-ups who believe they can outwit them!

As adolescence unfolded its complexities, the joy of walking began to wane. Early morning wake-up calls became a chore. Rebellion stirred within me, much like my defiance in school. The desire to embrace the typical teenage routine, to laze in bed or spend the day with

Nanna and Grandad surged within me. The allure of independence clashed with the structure of our family expeditions, leaving me yearning for a different kind of freedom.

During one such year, as we prepared for another navigation of the Dales Way, my mum, in a bid to streamline our gear, implored me not to pack a dress. The absurdity of her reasoning, suggesting it would add unnecessary weight and that there would be no occasion to wear it, fell on deaf ears. My rebellion took the form of wearing that carefully packed dress, symbolising my determination to carve out my path within the restrictions of our well-worn trails. Yearning to feel pretty, I emerged from our tent one evening in said dress, ready for the pub, much to the amusement of the adults. Like a secret shared, their chuckles echoed against the backdrop of the Dales. Feeling very smug that I'd managed to change without anybody realising, I felt grown up. Dad realised his little girl was changing.

One particular year, as boredom loomed over the walking routine, my love for cows and mischievous antics took centre stage. A field filled with cows and calves of every colour became my playground for amusement. With a playful shout of "Come on, cows! Come on, cows!", much to my mum's irritation, I incited a bovine mob as she hastened her step to escape the din. The term 'noisy cow' suddenly found a fitting context!

The hills echoed with the sounds of my adolescent spirit. In a moment of whimsy, lagging behind the walking group, I climbed a style, gazing at the meadow below.

Inspired by the upcoming school musical, *The Sound of Music*,[1] I jumped down from the style and overtook everyone else, singing at the top of my lungs, "The hills are alive with the sound of music!" A serenade to the countryside, a chorus that brought smiles to even the weariest of faces and bodies!

And then there were the hills, the undulating challenges that inspired and motivated my father. A promise of an ice cream van at the summit propelled me up those inclines, a tantalising prospect that made the climb more bearable! Dad, the king of mountains, imparted a lesson in pacing oneself – a lesson that transcended the hills and became a metaphor for life's ups and downs.

Our unconventional holidays, a testament to simplicity, revolved around a farmhouse nestled in the remote heart of the Dales. Shared with a few families, it welcomed us with the hissing embrace of two formidable geese at the cattle grid. The journey down a single farm track felt like a pilgrimage, leading us to a farmhouse frozen in time. Peat dug from the fells, crackling in the open fires, warmed our temporary haven. The barns, off-limits but whispering tales of farm life, stood as silent witnesses to our adventures.

As mentioned, Sundays took a turn when teenage restlessness set in. My plea to trade walking for potholing resulted in reluctant approval from Dad. The YSS bus shuttled us to the heart of the Dales. Stripped of our walking attire, we transformed into potholers – clad in snug wetsuits and helmets, and equipped with battery packs and lights. Eagerly awaiting our descent into the underground realm, I felt the thrill of stepping into the unknown – a world beneath our feet, waiting to unveil its secrets to the curious eyes of a teenage adventurer.

The pursuit of the extraordinary beckoned, and I answered its call with a spirit eager for the thrill of the unknown. Potholing, a dance with the depths of the earth, was distinct from caving[2] – a vertical ballet that demanded courage and an arsenal of specialised equipment. Soon, climbing rope ladders, abseiling[3] into the unseen, and breath-holding underwater passages became my routine. Each turn, each emergence into a vast chamber adorned with stalactites and stalagmites, was a revelation – a silent testament to Mother Earth unseen by human eyes for millennia.

Amid the enchanting landscapes of the Yorkshire Dales, hidden beneath the hills, lay the Three Counties cave system – an underground labyrinth stretching over 80 kilometres. Caving and potholing, once mere weekend activities, soon became a journey into the untouched realms of the earth. New cave sections awaited discovery, which I was eager to explore.

Abseiling, an essential companion to potholing, transcended from a necessary skill to a thrilling descent from cliff heights. The dangers inherent in this activity – where one descends using a friction device attached to the harness – added an edge to the adventure, but one not to be trifled with, given its history of fatalities.

Weekends with the walking and potholing group comprised adventure, intriguing escapades and boundless fun. Our unconventional attire, predominantly wetsuits, transformed coastal cave explorations and windsurfing in the Lake District into surreal experiences.

In my early twenties, the monotonous hum of daily life in the civil service was interrupted by an outward-bound team-building event in Castleton – a week of walking, caving and raft-building stirring memories of a bygone era. Tasks designed for team-building, including a night-time walk that led to pitching tents in the wilderness, became an unexpected challenge. Yet, even amidst stomach cramps and the unpredictability of a monthly cycle, the rugged beauty of the outdoors prevailed.

As life unfolded, celebrating my 50th birthday brought an exhilarating gift – a tandem skydive! Delayed twice by erratic weather, the third attempt became a moment suspended in time. The adrenaline rush of jumping from an aeroplane, soaring through the air with the earth unfolding below, will remain forever in memory – a reminder that life's most thrilling moments often lie beyond the bounds of our comfort zones.

A year later, revisiting the Dales Way minus the tent, I indulged in a more upmarket long-distance walking experience. Memories resurfaced, and the beauty of the Yorkshire Dales felt like a welcoming embrace – a homecoming that brought both a smile and a warmth within.

Reflecting on my life, there lingers a wistful regret for not pursuing a path as an outward-bound instructor. On the other hand, life – woven with the threads of family and the choices made – brings contentment. I impart to my children the wisdom of embracing life choices that resonate with their hearts, reminding them that regrets are but shadows of the past. From daring descents into the earth's depths, to soaring through the skies, the fortune of treasured memories remains a testament to a life lived on the precipice of extraordinary experiences.

Career
Fell Into a Bed of Roses – Cas Lass Came Good!

Embarking on a memoir of my career, I am peeling back the layers of a fascinating journey that started in the unlikeliest of places – Castleford in West Yorkshire, where dreams often had to find a way through the cracks. A school dropout with a modest plan to navigate through life, my path unfolded in ways I never could have foreseen. The story is about falling into a bed of roses, with thorns and blooms alike, and emerging triumphant as a "Cas Lass came good!"

My initial blueprint for life was straightforward: to finish college, to work in the civil service, and to start a family and be a full-time mum forever... Little did I know, life had a different script written for me. The civil service during the tumultuous miners' strike in Castleford became my training ground. Signing people on for benefits during a time of economic upheaval was emotionally demanding, a stark reality of families struggling to put food on the table. Amid punched tapes and pre-computer era challenges, I learned assertiveness that would become my lifelong companion. The miners' strike[4] of 1984 to 1985 marked a turning point in history, shaping not just my own career but the country as a whole.

Navigating the civil service at this time felt like walking a tightrope between policies and the harsh realities faced by families in Castleford. The strike was a seismic event that ripped through the entire UK, with profound effects on the political, economic and social landscape. It originated from the government's decision to close 20 coal mines, making 20,000 miners redundant. Mining communities faced economic devastation, leading to a national strike announced by Arthur Scargill, President of the National Union of Mineworkers. Initially peaceful, the strike escalated into clashes between picketers and police, and communities struggled to make ends meet amidst soaring unemployment.

The wonderful film *The Full Monty*[5], released in 1997, captured the essence of the struggles faced by many during this tumultuous period. Set in the steel industry rather than the mining industry, it is nevertheless an accurate portrayal of the economic hardship, the despair, the resilience of communities and the emotional toll of unemployment on families. It paints a poignant picture of the challenges faced by many people at the time, a window into the lives of individuals who were pushed to the brink, grappling with financial difficulties and societal expectations.

The characters' desperation and their eventual decision to take unconventional paths for financial survival resonated with the stark reality faced by many during that time.

This really hit home when a baby was left on the counter of our office; it was a cry for help – the family did not know where to turn or how to make ends meet. I never knew what happened to that baby and often wonder if it was adopted, like my son.

My first-hand experiences in the civil service emphasised the gravity of the socio-economic landscape and the impact it had on individuals and communities. My civil service journey, starting as an administrative assistant and rising to an executive officer, laid the foundation for what was to come. Life took unexpected turns during my children's growing years, leading me to take on part-time jobs, from being a dinner lady, to a hotel cleaner, to working in a plastics factory.

The turning point came when I stepped into a care home as an administrator, setting off a chain of events that would lead me to my current role as a senior executive in the health and social care industry, as detailed in *Memory Box 4*.

Embarking on my professional journey in the social care industry, I've worn many hats – from an operations manager supporting care homes, to a consultant turning around underperforming social care providers. The road led me not just nationally but internationally, collaborating with directors venturing into new territories, such as Norway and the Republic of Ireland, where I played a pivotal role in setting up master franchises.

These ventures weren't just professional conquests; they opened the door to a world of solo travel. Norway, with its captivating landscapes and high-tech cars, became the stage for my first foray into international exploration. The worry of missing connections due to flight delays initially tugged at my nerves, but I quickly learned to relinquish control over the uncontrollable, embracing the beauty of unpredictability.

Norway's allure is undeniable, with its breathtaking vistas and crisp, clean air. My driver, Mortan, introduced me to the wonders of self-driving technology, a rarity in the UK at that time. The journey from Oslo to the charming town of Arendal in the south unfolded in a sleek Tesla that showcased the future of transportation.

Arendal, a town immortalised in the Disney movie *Frozen*[6], added an unexpected touch of magic to my trip. Standing on a cliff with a winding path below me, I witnessed a live performance straight out of a fairy tale! Children dressed as the characters from *Frozen* sang their hearts out to a massive cruise ship in the harbour, creating a moment of enchantment that transcended the boundaries of age. Capturing this magical encounter, I live-streamed it on Facebook, sending a virtual postcard to my grandchildren. The joyous response asking, "Grandma, where are you? Can we come?" echoed the interconnectedness of our digital age, even though physical presence remained a distant wish.

As I reflect on these journeys, from the professional landscapes of social care to the literal landscapes of Norway, each step has been a blend of professional growth and personal discovery. The beauty of Norway, the novelty of a Tesla ride, and the unexpected *Frozen* serenade, became threads woven into my expanding narrative, reminding me that every venture, whether professional or personal, holds the potential for magic and connection.

Time To Myself
A Journey of Rediscovery After Divorce

The year following my divorce marked the beginning of a profound search for self. In the intricate roles of motherhood, grand-motherhood, and daughterhood, I had somehow lost the essence of ME along life's timeline. Confidence waned, and feeling unseen and invisible, uncertainty loomed over my future – the trajectory of my career, the possibility of homeownership, and the elusive concept of security. At 47, armed only with my salary and meagre pensions, I faced the daunting task of rebuilding.

In the interim, as mentioned, I found shelter under my mum's roof, in the familiar confines of my old bedroom. I grappled with the reality that lay before me – a clean slate, waiting to be filled with my own choices. The path ahead required diligence, hard work and a prudent approach to savings. Little did I realise, this juncture in life would become the rock on which I would build my resurgence.

Maintaining a work-life balance became my mantra. The spectre of burnout loomed large, urging me to tread carefully. Through a delicate dance of family, career and a budding relationship, I navigated the uncharted waters of post-divorce life. Simon, my partner, emerged as an unwitting ally and played a crucial role in my quest for self-discovery. He became a pillar of encouragement for my career aspirations, standing by my side as I made pivotal decisions.

The journey was far from easy. Emerging from a marriage that spanned most of my adult life to starting a new relationship was no fairy tale. It wasn't love at first sight; instead, it was a collaborative effort, a relationship where both parties had to work in tandem. Simon and I carried the baggage of our pasts, but together we unpacked and overcame the challenges, gradually cultivating a profound love.

Simon is a significant presence in my life. His unwavering support and encouragement became the backdrop against which I unfolded the layers of my new-found self. Navigating the complexities of blended families, we weathered the storm together. Simon harboured no aspirations to be a father to my children as he is the father of his own. My children embraced him for who he was – the person who brought joy to their mother's life and contributed to our shared happiness.

This new chapter of my life has been a nuanced blend of challenges and triumphs. Simon and I, bound not by blood but by choice, have sculpted a love that defies conventions. His acceptance into my life has been a testament to the enduring strength of love beyond the conventional norms. As I reflect on this journey of metamorphosis, I realise that I couldn't ask for more – a supportive partner, children who understand, and a life we've built together that continues to unfold with each passing day.

Acceptance

Liberation From Life's Grip – The Journey to Forgiveness and Happiness

For years, my mind concealed questions, silent echoes that reverberated through the corridors of my consciousness. Where was my child? How was he growing up? Why did parental decisions shape my path? The ghost of what-ifs lingered – what if I never saw my child? Why did my brother's life flicker out so young? These uncertainties, heavy as stone, crouched within the recesses of my mind.

Locking away memories seemed a shallow solution, a temporary refuge within the guarded chambers of my brain. Little did I know that this mental sanctuary wasn't the answer – it was simply an illusion, a pause button in the symphony of life. Armed with the clarity of the present, awareness dawned that things might have unfolded differently. Yet, the unpredictable path of life seldom yields to our foresight.

Unwanted memories[7] like ghosts sometimes intrude and our instinctual response is to build barriers, to fortify our mental fortress against their haunting presence. Over a century ago, Sigmund Freud hypothesised the existence of human defence mechanisms[8], such as repression and compartmentalisation – a psychological shield to manage and repel traumatic experiences and memories.

Recent advances in neuroscience have delved into the intricate workings of this defence mechanism, shedding light on the brain systems involved in 'deliberate' forgetting. Neuroimaging studies have mapped the terrain of our consciousness, revealing the possibility of intentionally blocking memories from our awareness.

To those grappling with the shadows of difficult times, I have been on a similar journey – I am here to hold your hand and share my narrative of personal growth. Life, an ever-shifting mosaic, often redefines our path through unexpected twists and turns. At the tender age of 15, innocence slipped through my fingers, replaced by the weight of premature adulthood. The vibrant outdoor enthusiast, who had once hoped to be an outward-bound instructor, witnessed the script of her life being inked in by parental decisions. This early divergence left an indelible emotional imprint, a silent companion shadowing my journey well into my fifties.

The act of writing these words serves as my therapy – an earnest attempt to transform my pain into some form of cohesion and understanding. My earnest wish is to spare others the agonies and reactive depressions that echoed through my own life. It's a testament to the resilience of the human spirit, an offering of compassion to those grappling with decisions that harbour enduring repercussions. Life is woven with threads of lessons, and this narrative stands as a humble stitch, urging understanding, forgiveness and, ultimately, the pursuit of happiness.

Unveiling the Mask: Beyond the Smile

In the theatre of life, I have played the role of a master illusionist. Expertly concealing my true emotions, I wore a smile like a well-rehearsed mask. However, behind the facade, I harboured a sea of unspoken feelings – tears, sadness and the weight of unfulfilled potential. Yet, I clung to this disguise, fearing that unveiling the raw truth would only ignite more negative emotions.

The art of concealing, however, is not the antidote. I am just as human as those around me, navigating the labyrinth of emotions with unique triggers that reveal a Pandora's box of experiences. To discover the authentic me, I had to embark on a journey of vulnerability, unearthing the most challenging chapters of my life.

Childhood, pregnancy, family death, bullies – these were the landscapes I traversed, the memories that haunted the recesses of my mind. Attempts to move forward proved futile; the ghost of the past lingered, waiting to be stirred by an unexpected trigger – a memory, a television programme, a throwaway comment.

The worst that could happen would be a cascade of tears, a shift in mood alien to my usually carefully crafted facade. Yet, in those vulnerable moments, I discovered the paradoxical strength of exposing my vulnerabilities. In acknowledging the pain, I found the first glimmer of healing. The journey to self-discovery, though daunting, illuminated the path towards authenticity, reminding me that being human means embracing both the light and darkness in equal measure.

Acceptance
Life-Changing – Forgiveness – Freedom – Happiness

Things began to shift when I opened up to someone. Oddly, I couldn't unveil my true self to those closest; they were too near, and I feared exposing my vulnerability. Thankfully, my friends guided me toward the right path. Asking for help is daunting, but once you take that leap, relief follows – the age-old adage "A problem shared is a problem halved" resonates. Asking doesn't get easier, but coping does. I've learned to live with my choices.

My choice was stark: let the past consume me, or find strength to navigate the darkness. Supported by my ex-husband, current partner, friends and children, I found that strength. Underage sex, resulting in a baby and adoption, and the hidden scars of reactive depression stemming from an underage pregnancy in a television show, and the unexpected death of my brother – all pivotal events in my life.

Today, none of these events dictate my narrative. I embrace them, thankful for the ability to talk openly and with understanding. Regrets linger, but I've accepted that I can't change the past.

I Am Who I Am

I have finally discovered the essence of who I am through the profound act of openness. My journey, marked by vulnerability and introspection, has transformed me from a closed book harbouring hidden health issues and a self-image I despised, into the authentic individual I am today. This metamorphosis didn't happen overnight but was an intricate process spanning years, an ongoing exploration of self that continues to unfold each day.

I chose not to let my health issues fester in the shadows; instead, I opened up to those around me, bared my soul and translated my experiences onto paper. In doing so, I found solace and connection, realising that my struggles could potentially resonate with others navigating their own difficult paths. Life could have unfolded differently, but I made a conscious choice to embrace change, and break free from the cocoon of a constrained self and emerge as the imperfect yet evolving person I am today.

Apologies become my compass when I err, and compassion guides my interactions with those facing challenges. I strive to be a steady presence for others, offering understanding and support in their moments of struggle. The trajectory of my life isn't fixed; I am open to exploring different paths, recognising that growth is a dynamic and continuous process.

I am an individual, far from perfection but wholly immersed in the journey of loving life. Each day on this planet is a gift, and I embrace it with gratitude, relishing in the richness of experience and the boundless possibilities that unfold as I continue to explore the depths of who I am.

Summary

Sometimes we do not believe that we will ever find ourselves. However, as you can see from this Memory Box, there are many stories, circumstances and actions that lead you to achieve what you considered impossible. If you find letting go challenging, you might like to consider the following.

Yvonne's Top Tips

- It is essential to find someone in whom you can confide and trust. Who is that person for you?

- We all have baggage – ask yourself why you are still carrying it around when it is stopping you from being you.

- Accepting yourself is a real challenge. Try writing down all the things you love about yourself, and the things you would like to change.

- Take one of the things you don't like about yourself and think about what you might do with great courage if you didn't care about what others thought about you. The positive feelings you think about yourself is incredibly empowering.

Memory Box 8: Letting Go

Time Waits for No Man, and Man Moves On

Life stories can teach us lessons, but we often have to repeat the lesson before understanding the sometimes undesirable result. However, there is a caveat. Despite learning to accept, we still hold on to memories that bring negative emotions, such as regret, jealousy and blame. The resounding negative memories played in our heads never seem trumped by the beautiful and joyful memories of achievement, precious moments and the feeling of love. It is a curious trait about being human that I have strived to deal with through the act of 'letting go.'

My ex-husband once came home from work and shared the heartbreaking news about a co-worker's son taking his own life. I had a familiar feeling in the pit of my stomach when he intimated that bullying was what the young boy experienced at school. Rob was distraught and decided that we needed to sit our girls down and talk to them about bullying. He was very much of the opinion that you should always stand up to bullies and that, as sisters, they all needed to look out for one another.

Emma, our eldest, was eight, Amy was six, and Jade was four. We kept the girls in the dark about why we were talking, as we believed they were too young to understand that someone had died. Emma was and is still the 'mother' of the three sisters; Amy, like myself, was quiet and didn't stand up for herself as a child.

A couple of days after this conversation, a call came from the school: Rob and I were summoned by the headteacher. It transpired that Emma had intervened with a girl who had been bullying Amy in the playground; Emma had witnessed it and took matters into her own hands. Emma was made to stand against the naughty wall and watch all the other children play. When asked by the headteacher why she had done it, Emma was adamant, "My dad told me to stand up to bullies, and sisters should always look after each other."

The headteacher was unhappy and told me that Emma had made matters worse. Now the head had two issues to address: not just the bully, but also Emma's intervention. Rob and the headteacher disagreed about Emma's behaviour; however, Rob wouldn't back down and was adamant the girls should always look out for each other. In the end, neither party backed down and therefore they agreed to disagree and Emma took her school punishment (I can't even remember what it was!). At home, we were pleased that the girls looked out for each other.

One of the biggest lessons from my life has been to consider my childhood and question what baggage I still carry around with me today. Exploring your past can be daunting, especially if you had a tough childhood. Seeking professional help can provide you with the guidance to confront it. However, the lessons and understanding of who you are become more apparent and straightforward as you journey into yourself.

Be careful of the fears from your childhood. It is all too easy to transpose them onto your children without intention, creating anxiety within them. I recall feeling anxious when Emma began high school. Of course, she ended up being fine, but I hadn't realised that I was thinking about my first lonely days at a new school and my fears as a young child, and was projecting my fears onto Emma.

Emma didn't know anyone at the school; she was tall with long, curly ginger hair, which meant she stood out in a crowd. We had recently moved to a new area where she had to travel to school by bus. I cried that first day when she left to catch the bus. Fear flooded my body, but I need not have worried. I had believed in talking to my girls about life, the good and evil, and through these conversations and my actions, we had given them life lessons.

An older girl, who was a well-known bully, had picked on Emma; with courage and a sense of right and wrong, Emma stood up to her. We all know bullies only continue their hideous behaviours when they believe they have power and control over someone weaker. Emma was strong and living with a different, more positive outcome; funnily enough, both the girls developed mutual respect and a friendship later in school! Behaviours can have both a positive and negative impact. Good behaviour can rub off on bullies too, thus creating a positive change.

One day, in my early twenties, I remember filling my car up at the local garage. To my horror, behind the counter was my junior school bully from all those years ago, as described in *Memory Box 1*. It was a strange feeling after these years. I didn't know if she would remember me, but I definitely knew her! To my surprise, she was friendly and pleasant. I remember thinking about what she had put me through, and that you must also live with the consequences of your childhood mistakes.

I walked out of the garage feeling proud of myself; I'd moved on. I had let go of all the bitterness, fear and resentment that had been brewing inside of me, causing me pain and a lack of confidence in my life. By letting go of the bullying, I regained my power, and that is a feeling that motivates me to move on and do better each day.

Dad, Are You Proud of Me?

I don't remember my father ever saying he was proud of me. This came to a head when emotions were running high after a heated argument between the two of us when I was trying to find my son.

At this stage, I was a mature adult, married with a family. I've always remembered my words, although the other parts of the argument remain buried.

I turned to Dad and said, "Are you proud of me?"

The look of surprise and then sadness on his face has always stayed with me.

"Of course I am," he said.

I replied, "You've never told me."

I'd taken him by surprise, so he then responded defensively with, "How do you think I feel knowing you think more of your grandad than you do of me?"

Well, that was a shock! We weren't meant to hurt one another in that argument, but we did. My response was simple: my love for my grandad was different to the love of my parents, and as a grandad himself, he should know that.

I am not sure where the need for my father's acknowledgement and recognition that he was proud of my endeavours and achievements came from. All I know is that I needed to hear it. However, what is vital to your self-esteem and growth is to remember that your parents' approval does not solely determine your worth as a person. You are valuable and worthy of love and respect, regardless of what others think.

As a parent, I am incredibly proud of all my children, their lives, and the values and morals that help them live life to the fullest.

Endings (Are Just New Beginnings)
Realisations

Whilst writing this book, I obtained my records from social services to see what had been written by the social worker in 1982 to 1983 at the time of my pregnancy and my son's adoption process. There was a drive within me that wanted everything I could have in writing; when something is in writing, it has more gravitas and finality about it. I needed to read the information and try to understand what had indeed happened. This time, I used the Data Subject Access Request.[1]

The following information is based on the ICO right of access and information[2].

Data Subject Access Request is commonly referred to as subject access, or SAR, and gives anyone the right to obtain a copy of their data and other information. It helps individuals to understand how and why others are using their data and to check it is being used lawfully.

Individuals can make a SAR verbally or in writing, including on social media. They do not need to use a specific form of words, refer to legislation, or direct the request to a particular contact. You can also ask a third party to make a SAR on your behalf.

In addition, you may also receive a SAR made on behalf of an individual online portal. Before responding, you need to be satisfied that the third party making the request is entitled to act on behalf of the individual.

Before responding to a SAR for information about a child, you need to consider whether the child is mature enough to understand their rights. If you are confident they can understand their rights, you should usually respond directly to the child. You may, however, allow the parent or guardian to exercise the child's rights on their behalf if it is evident that this is in the child's best interests. If a child is competent, they may allow someone other than a parent or guardian to make a SAR.

Getting the information this time took more work. I had to stand my ground and return to ICO several times, as they alleged had none of my records.

Eventually, the department sent what they call a 'controlled' file. Within the information, it was apparent my son's adoption was not my decision and that, although I had answered questions myself, social services thought coercion had taken place. And yet, they did nothing to protect my vulnerability! Reading the records was difficult, but I had an overwhelming desire to overcome it and move forward.

I've talked in *Memory Box 2* about the roles my parents played during the difficult time of the adoption and the choices they made, but time moves on. It's no longer about my parents; it's no longer about social services; this is now about me. I'm no longer the young bullied girl, the teenager who got pregnant, in a marriage that didn't stand the test of time, or overwhelmed by the depression brought on by the deaths of loved ones or unfortunate circumstances. I'm me, and I own everything I do as an adult.

I wrote this book because I have a story to share, something that others may relate to. I want to help others understand that we are all individuals; our life experiences make us who we are and embrace who we are. Acknowledgement only happens after some time. Getting where you want to be takes time, honesty and transparency. Does it matter what others think if you accept yourself and are true to yourself?

Writing this book has opened a Pandora's box of memories of all colours and shades. It has made me reflect. It's easy to forget about the feelings of others; until I started to write my story, I had never thought about the impact my teenage shenanigans would have on the direction of my parents and our family life; it's been so easy to think about me. Sometimes, the unsaid means more than any words spoken. I remained in the family home, standing on my own two feet. I wasn't thrown out onto the streets or disowned. I was still loved. Yes, decisions were made that had a lasting impact on the family, but ultimately, we remained a family.

I've learned to forgive. I've let go of any anger, resentment or bitterness that I may have had. That doesn't mean that what happened was okay. Forgiveness is something I need to do for myself; by doing this, I've healed, and in doing so, I've moved on with my life.

Forgiving people who have hurt you can be challenging, but forgiving yourself can be just as tricky. It is important to remember that learning how to forgive yourself is not a one-size-fits-all process.

Take a look at this article on the following website to give you some guidance: How to Forgive Yourself: Tips for Self-Forgiveness[3].

I acknowledge there will be times in my life when I am sad, when I am ill, when I have to sit back and watch my children make the same mistakes as I did. However, at this moment in time, I am thrilled with my life; it will always be a journey of learning, emotions, understanding, and acknowledging the happy times, the sad times and the everyday lifetimes.

It's strange how some memories are so clear whilst others become distant and hidden, locked away in a Memory Box until you find the key. Once you find the key, please remember that when the box is open, you either have to relock it or embrace what's inside. Sometimes, the key remains elusive; that was the case for me for years.

The Old Me

I needed to let go of the old me, but I also had to learn to embrace the old me as well as embracing the new me. In fact, it's not about the old or new me; it's about the person I am today. Was the old me that bad? I don't believe so, and at what point do I say that was the old me and this is the new me? The lines are too blurred.

What I have done is learnt from my mistakes, acknowledged where I could have done things differently or better, and apologised when I've offended or upset someone. I truly understand the circle of life, the innocence of children, the challenges of teenagers, and the fact that death can happen – either unexpected or expected. I understand the feeling of being both apprehensive and happy about bringing a new child into the world.

Knowing where I am now, I accept myself and look forward to whatever years I have left.

Summary

Be prepared for the emotions that come with opening your Pandora's box; it took me many years to find the inner strength to open mine. Be mindful that you might not be ready to deal with what you find...

Yvonne's Top Tips

- Tell those around you when something they do makes you feel proud.

- List your accomplishments; it is far too easy to forget the positive things we have done and focus on the negative things we have not done.

- Only you will know if you are ready to open your Pandora's box; don't let others railroad you into doing it – take your time.

Memory Box 9:
Time to Fly

Embracing the Future

As I reflect on the Memory Boxes of my life, the journey has been a roller coaster of highs and lows, with lessons etched into the fabric of each memory. My ex-husband's words, "He who tries hard and does his best is down the road like all the rest," echo in my mind, a reminder that, despite our best efforts, life may not always pan out as planned.

Being made redundant was a stark reminder that the path of life is unpredictable, and even the most dedicated can find themselves at a crossroads. Yet, I now carry with me the understanding that the value lies not just in the destination, but also in the journey itself. Trying our best, even when the outcomes mirror those of others, leads to personal growth and development.

I find solace in my work, a refuge that extends beyond a pay cheque. At a pivotal moment during a work-related event on change, we were prompted to examine our 'why.' My purpose crystallised: "To share my knowledge so that I can leave this earth knowing that I helped to improve the lives of others." It is this guiding principle that propels me forward, fuelling my dedication to both my career and my family.

Balancing the demands of work, family and the growing number of grandchildren has been an intricate dance. Hard-learned lessons taught me the perils of placing work above all else. Now, working remotely, I navigate the country, my home becoming a haven for both professional pursuits and personal moments.

The road is not without its bumps, though. The constant travel, the fatigue, the challenge of maintaining focus amidst the chaos of life. Simon, my partner, has adapted to the rhythm of my work-from-home days, even if it means passing by me with words unheard, masked by the hum of my earphones during a meeting. It's a dance of understanding and patience.

A humorous incident, immortalised in a Teams call, showcased the quirks of working from home. Simon, shirtless and cutting the grass in the background, unwittingly provided my colleagues with a surprise! It was like a clip from the TV drama, *Poldark*[1]! A moment that, in its hilarity, reminded me of the delicate balance between personal and professional realms.

Working from home, a trend accelerated by the global upheaval of the Covid pandemic has become both a boon and a challenge for many. I work from home but travel all over the country with my work; I relish the freedom, yet acknowledge the downsides. The constant need for focus, the blurring of boundaries between work and home, and the unexpected interruptions, such as my dog Bernie's protective barking during meetings, or when he wants his minute of fame and decides to jump up and put himself on view to everyone in the Teams meeting…!

But, despite the challenges, working from home remains my preferred mode. The freedom it affords, the flexibility to shape my workday, and the ability to be present for my family and grandchildren. As I contemplate the future, the dream of a continued balance, even in retirement, lingers – a life where my work and personal aspirations harmonise, leaving a legacy of shared knowledge and improved lives. The road ahead may be uncertain, but I step into it with a heart full of resilience and a spirit unyielding.

Embracing Life's Fragility

In the fabric of my family history, there is an indelible thread woven with the stark reality of my father's untimely death at the age of 57. He had a massive heart attack, a poignant reminder that intelligence does not necessarily mean you can see ahead. His lifestyle – marinated in the toxic cocktail of alcohol, smoking and a fatty diet – became the harrowing script of his end.

The echoes of his choices reverberate through my own life, a conscious effort to diverge from the precipice he faced. Weight is my struggle, but in that struggle, I find strength. I don't smoke, and while I may not be a fitness zealot, the golf course offers solace for both body and mind. My relationship with alcohol is tempered, a conscious decision to navigate a different path.

When health issues knock on my door, I don't cower in fear but rise to meet them head-on. A year on the NHS waiting list, a test of patience and resilience. Two options stretch before me like diverging roads – pay a substantial sum for private care, or patiently await my turn in the queue. Here, in the realm of waiting, patience battles restlessness. But I sit, determined to address the issue when the time is ripe, my voice carrying the weight of a woman who cannot wait any longer.

Work is not a choice, but a necessity. A phoenix rising from the ashes of divorce, I forged a new beginning at 47. A decade later, my financial security stands as a testament to my tenacity. I'm not reliant on others, and decisions about my financial future are solely mine. Pride swells within me as I bask in the ability to create memories, to take my family on holidays reminiscent of those I cherished as a child.

Dreams unfurl in the corridors of my mind. In a world where money is no object, retirement would find me on a golf course in a sun-drenched paradise with Simon, or traversing the globe together. Time would be the currency for moments with family – children and grandchildren gathered around. Retirement, a distant horizon, urges me to savour each day, a poignant reminder that the unexpected is always a whisper away.

The prospect of retirement is dreams of unabashed joy and graceful ageing. Jumping out of an aeroplane, feeling the rush of adrenaline, or scaling mountains to absorb the panorama of peaks and valleys below. Winter nights, the hush of snow outside, a warm fire, and the comforting embrace of Simon.

The breadth of my wanderlust extends beyond the limits of the known. Potholing in mysterious depths, feeling the sun kiss the shores of Italy, walking the undulating landscapes of the Lake District, or navigating the towering majesty of the Italian mountains. Where health allows, I'll travel, armed with a bucket list, accompanied by family, Simon and friends, or I'll venture into the solitude of solo exploration.

Contemplating the years to come, I see not a solitary figure, but a matriarch surrounded by a sprawling family – a tapestry of generations. In their eyes, I glimpse the reflections of Nanna and Grandad and see that their legacy lives on. Ninety-year-olds playing golf, not for the scorecard, but for the sheer joy of the game, inspire me. I want to be that testament to the enduring spirit of life.

My journey, with its twists and turns, has taught me that life is fragile, and every moment is an opportunity to craft a legacy of love, adventure and resilience.

The Dance of Self-Discovery

Walking away from the comfortable cocoon of my marriage was a seismic shift, a choice that reverberated through the lives of all involved – Rob, our girls, and me. The decision was not made lightly, and the echoes of its difficulty still linger. Yet, in the quiet aftermath, I found an unexpected gift – I found myself.

To be truly happy, I needed to forge a relationship with the woman in the mirror, to become intimately acquainted with the contours of my own soul. It required a kind of selfishness that society often misconstrues. Putting oneself first is not selfish[2]; it's a necessity, a cornerstone of well-being.

There's a pervasive myth that prioritising oneself is a selfish act. In truth, it's an act of self-preservation. Taking care of one's mental and physical well-being is not a luxury; it's a fundamental need. The guilt that often accompanies self-care is a heavy burden that I willingly discarded. It's okay to put oneself first; it's a declaration of self-love and acknowledgement of individual worth.

Just as the safety instructions on an aircraft instruct you to secure your oxygen mask before assisting others, so too must we tend to our needs first. Your body is the vessel that accompanies you on the journey of life; treating it with care is an act of love. Prioritising oneself is not a solitary pursuit; it is a collective responsibility we owe to ourselves and those around us.

The misconception that self-care is selfish stems from a societal narrative that values sacrifice over self-preservation. However, when you prioritise your needs, you become better equipped to contribute positively to the lives of those around you. Basic self-care rituals become crucial checkpoints in the tumultuous terrain of life, moments where you check in with yourself and reaffirm your value.

I embraced the journey of self-discovery, recognising that the path to happiness winds through the landscape of personal understanding.

As part of your new self-care regime, why don't you choose a physical activity, such as a brisk walk, a yoga session, or a favourite sport? Physical exercise releases endorphins, the body's natural mood enhancers. Setting boundaries is also integral to your self-care, as you affirm your value and convey to others that your time and energy are precious. Build in some down-time to your day. This self-advocacy fosters a sense of empowerment and reinforces the understanding that prioritising your needs is not selfish, but essential for your overall health and happiness.

In addition, taking time for mindful reflection and journaling is a powerful form of self-care that allows you to explore your thoughts, emotions and experiences. Carving out moments to reflect on your day, your achievements, and even your challenges, helps you gain clarity on your goals and values.

In the midst of recent lockdowns and the pervasive challenges of the present, self-care takes on added significance. It's a lifeline for the unmotivated, a balm for the depressed, a salve for the anxious. Now more than ever, practising self-care is an act of resilience, a testament to the importance of mental well-being in the face of adversity.

The delicate balance between kindness toward others and self-preservation is a dance many find challenging. While consideration for others is noble, it should not come at the expense of one's mental health. The journey to happiness involves finding the equilibrium between kindness to others and self-compassion.

As I navigated this labyrinth of self-discovery, I drew wisdom from diverse sources, acknowledging the invaluable insights from youngminds.org.uk, counsellorwhocares.co.uk, mentalhealthtoday.co.uk and blog.gratefulness.me. Each nugget of wisdom contributed to my evolving understanding – a dance of self-discovery that continues to unfold.

A Journey of Heart and Greens

In the quest to find myself, an odyssey that has strengthened me in every way, I've become an open book. I am unapologetically me – open, honest and transparent. I am not Wonder Woman; I am a woman who breaks, cries and loves. And in this intricate dance of self-discovery, I've unearthed a profound truth: to love others authentically, I must first love myself.

The year 2023 was not only marked by the continuation of my writing, but also by a daring challenge that beckoned me. Abi, one of my fellow golf companions, asked whether I would be up for the Macmillan Longest Day Challenge[3]. The mere thought of playing 72 holes, four rounds of golf, in a single day, might have given me pause in the past but not this year. The challenge held a poignant connection for me, echoing conversations with my grandfather in his final days, where Macmillan nurses provided solace and a space for acceptance.

Unclouded by doubts or reservations, along with the four other ladies in my golfing circle, we embarked on a mission to raise funds for Macmillan. With a shared commitment, we signed up, eagerly anticipating the arrival of marketing materials and sponsorship forms. However, disappointment set in as I perused the male-centric marketing material. Not one to be silenced, I wrote to Macmillan expressing my discontent, reminding them that ladies play golf and raise money too! An apology soon followed, accompanied by an unexpected bonus – a camera crew and photographer would document our journey for next year's challenge! A chance to capture our story in photos and video, a testament to the resilience of "women on the greens".

As we prepared for the challenge, setting our sights on an August date due to work commitments, a swell of emotions accompanied our heightened fundraising efforts. Doubts lurked in the quiet corners of our minds – were we physically fit for four rounds? Could we endure the mental stamina required? What if blisters became an unwelcome companion? Practical questions about meals, outfit changes, and the logistics of a 20-mile golfing endeavour loomed, threatening to derail our mission.

Yet, in the face of these uncertainties, I only had to conjure the memory of my grandfather. His courage fuelled my determination. The camaraderie amongst our group grew stronger as we faced the unknown together. The date neared, each swing of the golf club resonating with purpose. This challenge was not just about the greens; it was about resilience, connection and honouring a legacy. I was raring to go!

Triumph on the Greens

The morning of the challenge dawned, nerves and excitement woven into my restless night. The anticipation hung heavy as we converged at the club, golf warriors ready to embark on the Macmillan Longest Day Challenge. Family members bestowed well wishes, their support a comforting prelude to the journey that awaited us under the ascending sun.

We teed off, our swings slicing through the morning air. The promise of a beautiful summer sunrise accompanied us as we navigated the first few holes. Excitement and chatter filled the air, but the dew on the grass and the sun low on the horizon conspired against us, resulting in wayward shots and lost balls. The first round unfolded slower than expected, prompting concerns about the challenges awaiting us.

After the initial round, a brief respite awaited us in the form of traditional bacon butties, a welcome fuel for the golfing odyssey! The unexpected star of our day, the photographer, made his entrance. I had painted a picture for my fellow golfers, a vision of a discreet presence amidst the trees. The reality, however, was a different tale. The photographer was in our faces, demanding retakes in bunkers, urging for "more sand." His quest for the perfect shot was relentless, and even as we putted, he insisted on "more joy." The unexpected intrusion became a humorous backdrop to our day, and despite his constant presence, we somehow found ourselves forgetting he was there.

Round two concluded with homemade treats from supportive ladies, uplifting our spirits for the challenges that lay ahead. As we transitioned into round three, adorned in Macmillan-sponsored tops, the video crew joined the ensemble. Their cameras captured our shots, our determination writ large on film, and interviews probed our motivations for this relentless challenge. Family and friends joined us as caddies, providing a much-needed boost as fatigue set in. The camaraderie drowned out the weariness, and our mutual encouragement became a lifeline.

Round four, contrary to expectations, proved to be a crescendo rather than a struggle. The golf course became a canvas of support, with people cheering us on from all corners. The sun continued to grace us with its warmth, and our nourishment breaks were accompanied by the unwavering support of the camera crew, now integral members of our team.

As we approached the 18th tee, a united front with golf drivers raised, we recognised the magnitude of our achievement. The 18th hole unfolded, family and friends lining the fairway. With each swing, we inched closer to the culmination of our 72-hole journey.

As the ball sank into the 18th hole on the final round, tears flowed freely. It was 8:40 in the evening, the sun was setting, and I felt the presence of my grandfather, watching. In addition, Dad might not have been physically present, but the pride he would have felt echoed in my heart. Hugs, congratulations and Champagne ensued, the 18th green becoming a stage for our triumph. The journey had been arduous, but the victory was sweet, punctuated by the embrace of loved ones and the gaze of those who had joined us on this remarkable day.

The culmination of our journey marked the end of hole 72 and the realisation of a dream. We had done it! We eagerly await the video and the marketing material for next year, excited to be part of something bigger than ourselves. The journey was not solitary; it was a collective effort, a testament to the power of unity and determination. To those contemplating stepping outside their comfort zones, I say this: when the chance arises, don't overthink, just do it. The rewards may far surpass the challenges.

As the sun set on that August day, we completed our rounds, not just on the course but in our shared experience – a journey that mirrored the winding path of self-discovery, proving that sometimes, the most profound revelations unfold on the fairways of life.

Unveiling Me

The genesis of this book was shrouded in self-doubt, a reluctance to expose the raw and challenging emotions of my life. Each attempt to capture my story resulted in a few pages being quickly deleted, buried in the recesses of insecurity. The echo of not being good enough reverberated through my thoughts. Intellectually labelled as a school dropout, I wrote in the cadence of my Yorkshire accent, my words a reflection of my roots.

The turning point arrived in 2022, sparked by Colin, a godparent to one of my girls, venturing into the realm of authorship. Curiosity nudged me to reach out, posing the question that had lingered for years: "Where did you start?" Colin's guidance led me to a publisher, a pivotal figure in unravelling the knots of my locked Memory Boxes.

This journey has been a roller coaster, a plunge into the depths of self-exploration. It wasn't merely about writing a book; it was a voyage through memories and thoughts that had been shut away for years. The process of structuring my narrative became a therapeutic odyssey, a form of counselling with Brenda, my publisher, evolving into a mentor and confidante, guiding me through the labyrinth of expressing my feelings in writing.

In my initial perception, I envisioned narrating a story of a young girl navigating the complexities of having her baby adopted – a tale of life's inevitable undulations involving birth and death. However, the journey demanded more depth, urging me to excavate layers I had not anticipated that had been buried for years.

A self-imposed deadline loomed – 5th February 2023, my son's 40th birthday. Forty years since that hospital room witnessed the birth of my child, a poignant moment frozen in time. However, the emotional turbulence of my life rendered this deadline unrealistic, a testament to the complexities of my narrative.

Throughout the process, I have traversed the spectrum of emotions; crying and laughing, feeling mentally drained, yet finding solace in the cathartic act of storytelling. The book has become a vessel for healing, allowing me to speak freely about a past that once seemed insurmountable. The tears are a testament to my humanity, a reminder that vulnerability is a strength.

My initial belief that writing this book would mark the conclusion of my journey now appears remarkably short-sighted. It's not an endpoint but a beginning, an opportunity to openly share a life that resonates with the universality of human experience. If my words, my story, can touch even one person across the globe, then baring my soul was a worthwhile endeavour. The keys to those locked Memory Boxes, once elusive, now gleam in the light of revelation.

Authorship has been a profound teacher, imparting lessons on authenticity, resilience and self-love. It whispers in my ear not to fret about others' opinions, encourages me to seek help when needed, to take pride in my achievements, and to extend the same encouragement to those around me. It underscores the importance of self-love, recognising that without it, loving others becomes an uphill struggle. Most importantly, it ingrains the wisdom that life is precious; every minute matters – blink, and it's gone.

Summary

When life gives you opportunities, grab them and embrace every moment to the full. Don't be afraid to find yourself, to love yourself, and to give love freely and unconditionally back to others.

Yvonne's Top Tips

- You can't change the past, but you can and do have choices about your future; decide which baggage you want to carry and let the rest go.

- Give yourself something to look forward to, whether that is a holiday or time with your family; it doesn't matter what it is, as long as it means something to you.

- Have you ever thought "I'd like to do that," and then talked yourself out of it? Tell that little voice in your head to "jog on" and go embrace whatever it was that you want to do!

Memory Box 10: Unafraid To Be Me!

Gratitude Attitude

The Day I Nearly Died...

23rd December 2020

On 22nd December, Simon and I had been watching Nigella Lawson's cookery show on TV. Simon has a 'thing' for Nigella[1] as I'm sure others do! She is provocative with her language when pulling a recipe together and teases the viewer with the way she moves – anyway, whatever it is, he has the hots for her. Nigella had been making double chocolate chip cookies, which we don't normally eat, but Simon wanted to bake some the next day.

I awoke early and decided to go to the supermarket before the big Christmas shop rush started. It was dark and, not wanting to disturb Simon, I just grabbed whatever item of clothing I could. My intention was to dash in, buy the ingredients, and dash out again – nobody would see me at that time surely! God, I must have looked a sight. To put it simply, nothing I wore was coordinated and 'fashion police' would have locked me up! Getting my shopping as quickly as possible, I hoped no one would recognise me!

On the way back, I remember driving through the first village and thinking, "That lorry is out early and rather large to be coming through this village." I continued on my journey through the village along the back roads. I drove down the long lane, going over the dip in the road, but on reaching the T-junction at the end of the road, it was too late for me to drop my speed to a stop. The junction seemed to appear out of nowhere! I tried to slow down and, at the same time, turn right at the junction, but I was unable to.

The next thing I knew, a large ditch was looming toward me. Somehow the front of my car hit a tree and I toppled into the ditch, bonnet first, and the air bag went off. This all happened so quickly – my life literally flashed before my eyes; I genuinely thought, *This is it...*

With the rear of the car up in the air and the bonnet in the bottom of the ditch, I started to panic as there was smoke everywhere – was I going to go up in flames? I was desperately pulling at the car door, my heart beating out of my chest. I used all my strength but could not get the door open – it was stuck fast. The feelings of anxiety and panic were overwhelming.

Suddenly, a guardian angel appeared! Someone was shouting, asking if I was okay and whether I needed any help. A man managed to wrench the door open – and boy was I ever so pleased to see a friendly face! He helped extricate me from the car and I stumbled out of the ditch.

After thanking him for saving my life, I realised the smoke was from the airbag, not the car. Well, at least the car isn't on fire, I thought! Panic now over, I switched to 'organised Yvonne' mode. I needed to ring Simon, as he didn't even know I'd left the house. My rescuer rang Simon on his mobile but there was no answer. Of course! Simon no doubt assumed it was a wrong number or a bogus call. I had to use my mobile... which was currently in the car at the bottom of the ditch!

With my rescuer's help, I clambered back into the ditch and managed to get into the footwell of the car, retrieving my mobile.

On finally speaking to Simon, he thought I was joking! In the meantime, I had called the police to inform them of the accident and that my car was in the ditch. I also told them in no uncertain terms that I was unharmed as I didn't want them knocking on my mother's door as it would bring back memories of when my brother had been killed.

I felt that I didn't need an ambulance. Simon arrived shortly after and, of course, thanked my guardian angel. All this, and yet it was still only 6:30 a.m...!

Alone with Simon, I cracked and decided I had to go to the hospital as I was bleeding and it had to be checked out. But before getting into Simon's van, I asked him to get the food out of the back of the car. I didn't want anyone rifling through and taking the shopping!

However, on our way to hospital, I blurted out, "Oh no, I've done the worst thing ever!"

"Oh my God, what have you done?" Simon asked, imagining the worst.

"I've done what I always told my girls not to do… I've not got matching underwear on!" This was a family joke with the girls. I always told them to wear matching underwear as if something happened and they'd have to go to hospital, they would be so embarrassed that their underwear did not match. It was a delayed reaction. I was in shock and could only think of this inconsequential thought rather deal with the real gravity of the situation – after all, I could have been killed. Someone was looking out for me that day. Simon tried to console me, but I burst into floods of tears and started to shake uncontrollably.

Thank God, the A and E waiting area was empty as it was at the height of the pandemic when you were only allowed to visit the hospital in an emergency. But conversely it meant that Simon could not accompany me – I had to be on my own.

I was lying on the bed and my blood pressure was dropping. The nurse struggled to get blood from me. I had an electrocardiogram (ECG) which is a simple test to check the heart's rhythm and electrical activity.

Sensors were attached to my skin and used to detect the electrical signals produced by my heart. I was also taken for X-rays on my legs and wrists, but fortunately, there were no broken bones. Simon brought me an overnight bag but, of course, he could only drop it off at reception – no one was allowed to visit me.

I was kept in overnight, checked over thoroughly, and was questioned about what happened. I was battered and bruised but, fortunately, that was it – when I think about the what-ifs…

The strangest and hardest thing for me to deal with both then and now is my memory, or to be more precise, my lack of memory, of the accident. I do not remember anything from driving over the drop in the road, to when the T-junction just 'appeared'. I had a transient loss of consciousness – I blacked out. I had many different tests but the results came back as negative. I just could not remember anything.

I wasn't allowed to see any images of my car or the accident until I got home as it would have been far too distressing. The front of the car was completely crumpled from hitting the tree trunk prior to tumbling into the ditch.

I was watched over that day; it wasn't my time to leave this earth and for that, I'm extremely grateful. My thanks will always be to the man who rescued me and got me out quickly and calmly. I still have flashbacks of that morning when I drive down that road and pass the ditch, a reminder that things could have been different. I was extremely lucky.

I wasn't allowed to drive for six months to ensure that there were no further episodes. This imposed curfew was necessary but I was in a dark place, as I felt my independence had been taken away from me. After six months, I was given the all-clear and thankfully there have been no more incidents. I love driving, enjoying the freedom that it gives me.

Growing My Gratitude

Developing an attitude of gratitude has helped me to improve both my mental and emotional well-being. Although my son was taken from me without my true understanding of the consequences, once I'd met him and realised that he'd had a good upbringing and that he was happy, I too was happy. I wrote to the social worker to thank her for ensuring my son was adopted by a couple whom she knew to be kind, caring and loving. I will be forever grateful to her for this act of kindness.

There are many other ways that you can improve your mental and emotional well-being. Try and find something that is right for you and fits in with your time. Buy a special notebook or journal in your favourite colours and make a note of what you are grateful for each day. This is your Gratitude Journal.

In addition, make an effort to say thank you to the people in your life who have had a positive impact; it could be a simple thank-you note, a text message, a voice call, or a face-to-face thank you. Any of these actions will make someone feel loved and valued.

Furthermore, it is a two-way street – you will feel loved and valued as well.

What I like to do is be grateful with a positive focus on what I have, rather than a negative focus on what I don't have.

Try and embrace every day and every moment, as one never knows what is around the corner. Developing an attitude of gratitude does not come naturally to everyone – you need to commit time and effort until it becomes second nature. But even if you feel it is not for you, keep trying – the rewards you will receive in terms of joy and positivity in your life will be abundant.

Mindfulness

Mindfulness is the practice of choosing to pay attention to the present moment using a calm, kind, non-judgemental approach. As humans, we can be mindful, but much of the time we forget because we get distracted by thoughts which take our attention away from the present and we become regretful about the past or fearful about the future.

When the mind is elsewhere, we often revert to autopilot mode, where we're not fully conscious and actions and decisions are taken automatically using the unconscious part of the brain. Whilst that can be helpful, either to save time, or even to save us from danger, we can miss out on truly experiencing life as it happens, and miss important signals from the body.

By waking ourselves up to the present, we can understand ourselves better and choose how we respond to life's ups and downs. Bringing kindness to our choices helps us to develop self-compassion and, ultimately, compassion for others.

Mindfulness has been the subject of much scientific research, particularly in the last 10 years. The Oxford Mindfulness Centre[2] has been at the forefront of Mindfulness-Based Cognitive Therapy (MBCT) research, innovation, teaching and training since it was founded in 2008. It is a collaboration between the University of Oxford Psychiatry Department and the Oxford Mindfulness Foundation (OMF), a UK-registered charity.

MRI scans have been used to see how the brain changes when people practise mindfulness, offering some fascinating results. Evidence suggests that certain areas of the brain may either shrink or grow in response to regular mindfulness practice. Here are a couple of examples.

- Mindfulness and stress. After practising mindfulness, the grey matter in your brain's amygdala – a region known for its role in stress – can become smaller.

- Mindfulness and creativity. The prefrontal cortex is the area of your brain responsible for things like planning, problem-solving, and controlling your emotions. The grey matter in this area can become thicker after practising mindfulness, showing increased activity in these areas of thought.

- Mindfulness and memory. An area of the brain known as the hippocampus helps your memory and learning. This area too can become thicker after practising mindfulness.

See 'How does mindfulness affect the brain?'[3] in the References section.

As seen in the above referenced BUPA study, there is clear evidence that those who practise mindfulness regularly have measurable differences in brain structure compared to those who do not. These differences can result in improved concentration, decision-making, memory and emotional intelligence.

In addition, numerous benefits become apparent when you practise regularly, particularly when you compare it to periods when you do not. These benefits include better and deeper sleep, reduced anxiety, improved response to stress, feelings of happiness and more positive relationships.

We can train ourselves to be more mindful more of the time, using mindfulness practices and integrating mindfulness into our daily lives. Start with something simple. You could try meditating on the same day every week for a month, or every day for a week. This involves sitting quietly for a while, choosing an 'anchor' to focus on, such as your breath or mantra, which you can come back to whenever your busy mind wanders. It is different to some other types of meditation that have a goal to achieve, such as emptying the mind or simply relaxing, which I personally struggle with.

A mindfulness meditation is not trying to achieve a different state, but simply to 'just be' with things as they are. When you notice that you're distracted, have a busy mind, or an emotion becomes apparent, simply allow it to be there and choose to gently redirect your attention back to the anchor. The anchor could be feeling the breath, sensations in the body, or noticing the senses.

There are other ways to bring mindfulness into your day in lots of different ways. Here are some examples that I have gleaned from my great friend and golfing pal, Kate Osborne[4]:

- Instead of pressing the snooze button when you wake up, use the extra couple of minutes to open your eyes, look around the room, feel your breath, and make an intention for the day.

- Stand tall with your shoulders back once you have finished in the shower and feel the water running off your body.

- Readjust your posture during meetings or when you're driving. Your breathing will become deeper and you will become more alert.

- Notice whether your breath reaches your stomach or sits higher up in your chest, and whether your shoulders are tense or not – this indicates how stressed or relaxed you might be. Make wide circles with your shoulders to try and release the tension.

- Take a moment periodically through the working day to notice if you have crossed your legs – uncross them so they don't restrict the blood flow in your legs.

Living Life on YOUR Terms

What does it mean to live life on your terms? Why is it so important? Who do you need to become to live life on YOUR terms? How does it benefit you?

I live life on my terms; however, that doesn't mean that I'm neglectful of those around me. On the contrary, I'm more mindful of how I make them feel.

As children, we are given rules and boundaries which help teach us how to react to situations. When I was a child, if it wasn't appropriate to laugh when someone tripped up, I'd be given a firm glare by my parents, or if the tears were turned on, I'd be told to wipe them away.

When I became a wife and a mother, everything was now about my family. The decision made couldn't be simply about what I wanted, as to do so would have an impact on those closest to me; my husband and my young children growing up. At no point did I ever think anything was lacking. Making these decisions on a collective basis for the good of the whole family didn't sadden me – in fact, it was the opposite; I was happy and so was my family. However, reflecting on family life now, all these years later, I was living life through the prism of my husband and children.

I'm now in a different stage of my life where for the first time life is lived on my own terms. It was extremely challenging at first – as a wife and mother, I was almost programmed to think about others when making choices and decisions. I have had to dig deep and find myself. Whilst on the journey of finding myself, I've realised that I'm unafraid, unstoppable and unapologetic.

I am not scared to question or speak up for myself. If I don't believe something is right, I will say so; however, I will always try to do so in the right way. When I am at work in a professional environment, the discussion will be undertaken in a calm, collected and courteous manner. In my personal life, I am always mindful of people's feelings.

I'm no longer afraid to open up and to have those 'difficult' conversations. There is nothing worse than something festering in your heart or your head because you have not mustered up the courage to confront it. Leaving my job as a CEO was one of the hardest decisions I have ever made. I loved my job but realisation hit home that I was working for someone whose values were very different to mine. Once again, I was torn; this time I made my decision to leave after confronting the owner about his methods. It turned out he wanted someone (i.e., me) to be the face of the business whilst he was the puppeteer pulling the strings behind the scenes.

I knew it was the right decision and now my life is so much happier as a consequence. It has taken me a lifetime to get to this point, a lifetime of learning, questioning and reflection.

I'm unstoppable but I don't have a cavalier attitude – I am not one that rides roughshod over others, or that carries on without any concerns about those around me. I'm unstoppable because I have a **PURPOSE** with a full life, family, friends, and a relationship with someone who supports me to be me. I'm not afraid to take risks, as long as I have taken the time to assess why I'm doing it, what I need to do, and what the outcomes could be.

I will always give something a go and try something new, taking myself out of my comfort zone. For example, when I took on a tandem skydive, as mentioned earlier on, or continued to push myself in my career.

When I have not been happy in my professional life, I have asked myself whether I truly enjoy getting up every morning. If not, then what am I going to do about it? There's no point in complaining, being miserable and staying in a job 'just in case'. One has two choices; stay put and just get on with it, or plan a departure and risk assess the consequences of said departure. The outcome is to simply find another job.

I'm unapologetic for being me. This does not mean I'm heartless and unfeeling. It means that I accept who I am and the mistakes I've made. I don't need to apologise to my children for my marriage ending. They see now that I am happy with myself and by being happy with myself, I have all this love to give. No one should need to apologise for being themselves, unless, of course, they are rude or offensive. It is odd how many of us constantly feel the need to apologise – for instance, when someone knocks into us as we are walking down a busy street. Even when we are not at fault, we tend instinctively to say "Sorry!"

Through my journey and the process of putting pen to paper, I have discovered that I have several non-negotiables which have helped me to take control and make my choices.

I feel that honesty is the foundation of any relationship – be it with your family, spouse or friends. Without honesty, there is no trust or respect. Dishonesty in a relationship leads to deceit and mistrust, and it is likely that the relationship will not last. Have you ever checked your partner's mobile phone because you don't trust them? If yes, you need to be brutally honest with yourself and ask yourself whether this is the right relationship for you – is it worth you continuing it? If the answer is a resounding yes, then stop checking the phone, and have an open and honest conversation. Be prepared for the conversation to go either way – the relationship will either work or it won't.

Accepting myself is another non-negotiable; nurturing myself and being unafraid of being me. By taking time out for myself, I am more able to give back to those around me. There's nothing worse than a tired, snappy Yvonne, as Simon knows! Sometimes I don't see it, but Simon clearly does. When he says, "You'd argue that black is white and vice versa," then I know at that point I need to take myself off to bed for some early nights!

I ensure that I have a work/life balance to help me with my third non-negotiable, which is finding time for my family. In this day and age where we all work, this can sometimes be difficult so weekends are the times that I try to catch up in person.

If I'm not able to, I will always video call. Apart from seeing my grandchildren in person, the next best thing is a video call. Being able to see them when I'm working around the country stops me from feeling I'm missing out. Seeing their loving, mischievous faces around the breakfast table all saying, "Love you, Grandma!" always fills my heart with love and joy.

I work hard and play hard but like to get away every three to four months to help me switch off from work. I need to make the effort and find time to do this, otherwise I feel like I am 'on call' all the time and constantly check my work phone for messages and updates. On the last working day before my holiday, I clear as many emails as possible, put my 'out of office' on and then switch the phone off. It is a true feeling of relaxation and elation! I leave the phone at home, as the breaks are my time with Simon, and with friends and family. In addition, I've learnt not to switch the phone back on until the morning I go back to work.

Over the years, there have been a couple of times when the final day of my holiday has been ruined because I've switched the phone back on too early, destroying my holiday mood and often tainting the whole holiday. Holidays are precious to me from my childhood when wonderful memories were made – I want my children and grandchildren to feel the same.

Having 'me' time keeps me going. Yes, of course, I am a daughter, mum, grandma and partner, but most importantly, I am me. If I don't want to do something, I will say so; if I don't say something and then go along with it, I will be grumpy with everyone and be furious with myself, but will only have myself to blame. I will compromise, but if the compromise makes me unhappy, then I'm sorry, but I'm not doing it.

I used to play golf in all conditions but today I'm a fair weather golfer. There's no fun in hacking a ball around the golf course when the rain is pelting down! However, if it's dry but cold, I'll get wrapped up and go and play. There's no point in playing if my head is full of worries or work issues, as all it does is stop me from concentrating, enjoying the company, focusing on my game and taking in the beautiful surroundings.

When on holiday, my 'me' time is immersing myself in a book. I start reading on the plane and continue whenever I'm around the pool or on the beach. I make a conscious effort to switch off from everything around me when reading.

Today, I'm thankful every day for my life; however, as you have read over these pages, this was not always the case. I took being made redundant personally and was devastated, but I picked myself up, got another job and moved my career forward.

Suffering the miscarriage, made me feel as though I was being 'punished' for giving my son away, but it was a blessing in disguise as it revealed the abnormal cervical cells and, fortunately for me, there was treatment.

When my brother was killed, his death and the death of his two colleagues led to major changes in the tower crane industry, making it much safer for everyone, so at least something positive came out of it.

Often, it's so easy to think of the negatives, but if one flips the lens, there is usually, if not always, something positive that can be found, even in the darkest moments.

Finding Joy in the Smallest of Things

Joy is the state of an intense feeling of happiness and satisfaction. It is also about success, pleasure, delight and gratitude.

Sometimes it is so easy to think about what could have been or what should have been – the feeling of regret, of what-ifs… Being in that mindset can drag you down. I try my best to think of what I have now and the joy of all the things that I have experienced, that I have made possible: my family, my ex-husband, my children and my grandchildren. I also reflect on the happy times, however short they were, with my grandparents, my father and my brother.

I had a wonderful childhood, doing things that other children in those days never did, let alone children today in our phone and screen-obsessed society. I lived a life outdoors, camping under the stars, walking, potholing, and swimming in lakes and the freezing North Sea. I saw the stars at their clearest in places where there was no light pollution, where in a flash, a shooting star would pass by and then was gone, reminding us all of the transiency of life.

As a family, we did things together. Yes, my dad drank more than he should, but that didn't stop him from doing the things he loved and spending time making arts and crafts with his grandchildren, or taking us all on camping holidays. So what if my dad went to the pub? I realise now he was a functioning alcoholic but that didn't make him a bad person! These are the times that I remember with great affection – the happy times, the innocent times, when I was free and full of joy. I was loved, am still loved; I give love to others and love myself.

Today, joy can be found in the smallest of things. On a recent visit to Scotland, I was so excited at seeing my first-ever red squirrel at the age of 56! I was like a small child, overcome with excitement, trying to keep as quiet as possible, so as not to scare the squirrel away!

A few years ago, a pair of otters took up residence in the lake behind our house. I watched them swimming and enjoying themselves and was enraptured by the whole scene. I have always had an affinity with otters. Shut away in my keepsakes is a limited edition pencil drawing of an otter that I was given in my teens. Seeing a pair so close, enjoying the winter sun and frolicking around the lake playfully was a dream come true for me.

I love to watch my grandchildren do something new and see how proud their parents are when the children learn a new word, recite their times tables, or master something physical like riding their bikes. I remember those feelings when I was a parent; I couldn't wait to tell my husband or parents what new thing the children had done that day.

Often, I find joy in the simplest of things. Whilst driving, a song will come on the radio that I adore, so the volume gets turned up and off I go, belting out the tune! (I'm completely out of tune but who cares?!) At that moment, I'm in my own world, driving along and loving life. I have made a list of songs that are my favourites and often play them. Some might find this morbid, but I have already made a song list for my funeral…

Finding joy will be different for everyone: it might help to write things down and make a list of what brings you joy. Is it sitting quietly after a long day at work with a cup of tea? Or having a big family gathering? It could be taking a long walk with your partner, your dog or a friend, or looking after the children in your life. It could be time to yourself to practise your favourite sport or hobby, go to the cinema, or simply pamper yourself.

Today, not only am I an executive in the health and social care industry, but I have also become an author! The process of writing has opened up so many memories – both good and bad. My Memory Boxes have been unlocked and I have not been afraid to reach deep inside, no matter how painful it was to do so.

Beginning the journey in what seemed like a never-ending, dark and gloomy tunnel, with no doors or windows, I could just about see a small chink of light but it was so far away. I entered the tunnel years ago, but each time I managed to find a space to escape into the light and air, as it was too hard to go all the way, open up the Memory Boxes, and write anything down. Surely no one would want to listen to me and read my story?

Taking the difficult decision to re-enter the tunnel, and forcing myself not to look back or to try and escape again, was tough. At times the tunnel remained dark and got even darker, but gradually the chink of light at the end got larger and closer. Along the way, the process of writing helped me to heal. I revisited old wounds and pulled off the sticking plaster, giving each wound air to breathe and repair. Connecting with my inner child and my soul reminded myself how happy my childhood was and how I was very much loved, not only by my grandparents but also by my parents.

Summary

If you are going through tough and challenging times, please do reach out to others for help. Remember, this is not being weak – in fact, it is quite the opposite! To admit needing help, to show your vulnerability, takes great courage, strength and resolve. You will find your light at the end of the tunnel, just as I did.

Yvonne's Top Tips

- Life is often one step forward and two steps back, and the path you thought you wanted to follow may not necessarily be the right one. Be open to other ways of thinking and see where this takes you – you might be quite surprised!

- Every action causes a reaction; don't let others influence the true 'you'.

- Find a purpose, something fulfilling to do; learn a new skill, volunteer for your local charity, or set yourself a goal to achieve within a certain time frame.

- You are **not** your parents; you are a unique individual in your own right.

Epilogue

Dear Reader,

You have seen snippets of the 'Cas Lass' that has lived and continues to live, the 'Cas Lass' that came good! I don't think of myself as a natural author: I'm just someone who had a story to tell of the ups and downs of life – childhood, being a teenager, pregnancy, love, death and health. The path I have travelled hasn't been a straightforward one, but whose is? My life has been filled with twists and turns, good days and bad days, but putting pen to paper has been a journey of recollection and reflection, embedding the person I am today.

Would I change it? I'd be a liar if I said no as, of course, there are some episodes I would change but I can't, so I'll have to let it go. I'm now content, as I've finally found 'me'. It has taken a long time but that's okay – it's better than okay, it is exhilarating!

If my book helps even one person to think about their choices and how to navigate their life, then it will be a job well done. I started writing for purely selfish reasons – to help me heal. Has the process of writing healed me? YES!

So what is next for me moving forward? What does my future look like? Unfortunately, I do not have the answer. I would like to give talks to help support others who need a helping hand or a friendly buddy on their life's journey. There is no point keeping all my learning to myself.

Do you have a story to tell? Why not give it a go? You might be surprised with what you find out about your inner self.

Note to My Younger Self

You Are Loved. I might not have always thought it, but my parents loved me very much. I probably wasn't the best behaved and clearly didn't follow the rules... but like all children, rules are there to be broken, aren't they?!

Know Yourself. It is vital to know yourself; once you do, you'll understand what your values are, what boundaries you have, and why you need to have them in the first place. Knowing yourself will give you greater happiness.

Love Yourself. How many of us can say that we love ourselves? I was brought up in a society where loving yourself meant you were big-headed or had ideas above your station. Times have changed with the focus on mindfulness and well-being. Embrace the change, find your inner self, love the person you are, and show love to those who mean the world to you.

Above all, Be Yourself. Show your emotions – laugh, cry, lose your temper. Don't wear a mask to suit those around you; let them accept you for who you are. Move away from so-called 'friends' who lead you down the wrong path, and ensure that you break the hold on unhealthy relationships. Never forget that you are your own person.

References and Further Reading

Chapter 1

1. *My Bonnie Lies Over the Ocean*, traditional Scottish folk song, published by composer Charles E. Pratt in 1881 under the pseudonym H.J. Fulmer (or Fuller) and J.T. Wood.

2. *The Wizard of Oz*, directed by Victor Fleming (1939), produced by MGM, based on L. Frank Baum's 1900 book, *The Wonderful Wizard of Oz*.

3. 'Characteristics of Bullying Victims in Schools', Rosie Green, Aleks Collingwood and Andy Ross, National Centre for Social Research, July 2010. https://assets.publishing.service.gov.uk/government/uploads/system/uploads/attachment_data/file/182409/DFE-RR001.pdf

4. BBC News: 'What's it like to be a latchkey kid?'
    Perminder Khatkar, 26th May 2010 http://news.
    bbc.co.uk/1/hi/magazine/8704827.stm

Chapter 3

1. *Tom and Jerry*, created by animators William
    Hanna and Joseph Barbera for MGM. Tom and
    Jerry made their debut in the theatrical short *Puss
    Gets the Boot* (1940) and were a hit with audiences.

2. *Rugrats* is an American animated television series,
    created by Arlene Klasky, Gábor Csupó and Paul
    Germain for Nickelodeon. The series premiered on
    11th August 1991 and was popular in the UK.

3. *The Flintstones* produced by Hanna-Barbera
    Productions, the animation studio founded by
    Academy Award-winning producers William Hanna
    and Joseph Barbera.

4. *Brookside* written by Phil Redmond, produced
    by Mersey Television for Channel 4. Broadcast
    on Channel 4 from 2nd November 1982 to 4th
    November 2003.

Chapter 4

1. Health & Safety Executive
    https://www.hse.gov.uk

2. *Dancing Queen* written by Benny Andersson, Björn Ulvaeus and Stig Anderson, produced by Benny Andersson and Björn Ulvaeus. Sung by ABBA, released as the lead single from their fourth studio album, *Arrival* (1976).

3. 'Reactive Depression: Symptoms, Causes and Treatment Options' https://mentalhealthdaily.com/2014/03/25/reactive-depression-symptoms-causes-treatment

4. *Coronation Street*, produced by Granada Television, ITV Productions and ITV Studios. Broadcasted on ITV since 9th December 1960.

5. The After Adoption support group is no longer available.

6. BBC News: 'Mothers demand apology over forced adoptions,' Duncan Kennedy, 25th May 2021 https://www.bbc.co.uk/news/uk-57231621

7. *The Story of the Dragonfly* by Doris Stickney, Pilgrim Press, 50th Anniversary edition, 2022. First published under the title *Death in Colloquy* (December 1971), the story was revised and expanded in 1982 to become the bestselling *Waterbugs and Dragonflies: Explaining Death to Young Children*. https://achildofmine.org.uk/the-story-of-the-dragonfly/

Chapter 5

1. The Great British Care Awards
   https://www.care-awards.co.uk

2. Imposter Syndrome, Stephen Eldridge, 13th January
   2023. https://www.britannica.com/topic/imposter-
   syndrome

Chapter 6

1. 'Pregnancy: What is a healthy weight?', British
   Nutrition Foundation Information Review
   Panel, June 2015, https://www.nutrition.org.uk/
   nutrition-for/pregnancy/

2. BBC News: 'How the contraceptive pill changed
   Britain,' Rebecca Cafe, 4th November 2011
   https://www.bbc.co.uk/news/uk-15984258

3. Urinary incontinence. Last reviewed 15th June 2023.
   https://www.nhs.uk/conditions/urinary-
   incontinence/

4. Vaginal mesh, Faculty of Learning, NHS Resolution,
   24th January 2024, https://resolution.nhs.uk/vaginal-
   mesh/

5. Menopause. Last reviewed 17th May 2022.
   https://www.nhs.uk/conditions/menopause/

6. Post-menopausal bleeding. Last reviewed 22nd May 2023, https://www.nhs.uk/conditions/post-menopausal-bleeding/

Chapter 7

1. *The Sound of Music*, musical by Richard Rodgers and Oscar Hammerstein II, first staged 1959.

2. Caving & Potholing, Yorkshire Dales Guides https://www.yorkshiredalesguides.co.uk/caving-potholing

3. 'Climb skills: how to abseil,' Jonathan Garside, 14th March 2016, British Mountaineering Council https://www.thebmc.co.uk/climb-skills-abseiling

4. BBC News: 'Why UK miners walked out and how it ended,' Georgina Morris, 2nd March 2023 https://www.bbc.co.uk/news/uk-england-68244762

5. *The Full Monty*, directed by Peter Cattaneo, 1997, screenplay by Simon Beaufoy.

6. *Frozen*, directed by Chris Buck and Jennifer Lee, 2013, and produced by Walt Disney Animation.

7. 'How to forget unwanted memories,' Louise Morales-Brown, Medical News Today, 22nd December 2023, https://www.medicalnewstoday.com/articles/251655

8. Sigmund Freud, *The Neuro-Psychosis of Defence*, German edition, 1894, in *The Complete Psychological Works of Sigmund Freud*, Volume 3: *Early Psycho-Analytic Publications* (1893 – 1899), English edition translated and edited by James Strachey, Vintage Classics, 2001.

Chapter 8

1. Right of Data Subject Access, https://ico.org.uk/for-organisations/uk-gdpr-guidance-and-resources/individual-rights/individual-rights/right-of-access/

2. ICO, the Information Commissioner's Office, https://ico.org.uk/for-organisations/uk-gdpr-guidance-and-resources/individual-rights/individual-rights/right-of-access/

3. *How to Forgive Yourself*, Keendra Cherry, Very Well Mind, 5th December 2023, https://www.verywellmind.com/how-to-forgive-yourself-4583819

Chapter 9

1. *Poldark* is a British television series which first aired in the UK on 8th March 2015. The series is based on the novels of the same title by Winston Graham, and was written and adapted for the BBC by Debbie Horsfield.

2. 'Putting yourself first is not selfish,' Aarushi Tewari, *Gratitude – the Life Blog*, https://blog.gratefulness. me/put-yourself-first/

3. Macmillan Longest Day Challenge, Macmillan Cancer Support, https://longestdaygolf.macmillan. org.uk

Chapter 10

1. Nigella Lawson, English food writer and television cook, https://www.nigella.com

2. The Oxford Mindfulness Centre, https://www. oxfordmindfulness.org

3. 'How does mindfulness affect the brain?' by Caroline Harper, 14th October 2021, https://www. bupa.co.uk/newsroom/ourviews/mindfulness-my-brain

4. Kate R Osborne, Mindfulness Trainer and Results Trained Coach, https://www.linkedin.com/in/kate-r-osborne/

Acknowledgements

Opening myself up to write this book has been so very difficult, but I want to express my gratitude to Colin for guiding me to a great publisher who helped me through the process.

Writing this book has been a journey of over two years, digging into the depths of my memories. Brenda, my publisher, has been there every step of the way playing a crucial role in making this book a reality whilst being my mentor, a voice of encouragement, and understanding my need to support others who may find life difficult at times. Without the support of Brenda, this book would not exist.

I want to acknowledge my mum and express my love for her. Although it was difficult to understand her reasons at times, I now realise that self-reflection and understanding oneself is crucial. Forgiveness is not the key, but being true to yourself and being able to live with yourself is.

I am grateful to my son's parents for providing him with the love and care that I couldn't.

To my children and grandchildren, you are my world; words cannot express how much I love you all.

Simon, thank you for supporting me in everything I do. Without you, I wouldn't have found the true me.

Yvonne

About the Author

Yvonne Tomlinson is an award-winning trainer, business executive, author, and a loving mum and grandma.

At the age of 15, Yvonne dropped out of school with uncertainty about her future. After a failed marriage and career path that wasn't mapped out, Yvonne became a hard-working businesswoman, standing on her own two feet, turning around underperforming care and homecare businesses, and growing an international franchise business.

Yvonne has learned the hard way and now ensures she has a work-life balance that involves spending time with her family and partner. A leisurely game of golf can soon become competitive, especially when a win is in sight!

Yvonne is proud of her down-to-earth Castleford roots. As someone once said to her, "The Cass lass came good!"

Connect with Yvonne:

www.linkedin.com/in/yvonne-tomlinson-59498537

yvonnetomlinson67@hotmail.co.uk